PHARMAGEDDON:
A Nation Betrayed

PHARMAGEDDON:
A Nation Betrayed

**A NATIONAL TRIAL LAWYER REVEALS AN
INDUSTRY SPINNING OUT OF CONTROL**

*Stephen A. Sheller Esq.
with New York Times best-selling author
Sidney D. Kirkpatrick*

Visit www.ANationBetrayed.com for updates, news, video, and more.

© 2016 Cape Cedar Media
All rights reserved
ISBN: 0615893163
ISBN-13: 9780615893167
Library of Congress Control Number: 2013951347
Cape Cedar Media, Norfolk, VA

The main reason we take so many drugs is that drug companies don't sell drugs; they sell lies about drugs.

—Dr. Peter Gøtzsche, professor of clinical research design and analysis and director of the Nordic Cochrane Center

Introduction Death by Prescription   xi

Chapter 1   *Bush v. Gore*: How the Fox Got
in the Henhouse   1
Chapter 2   Your Prozac Is in the Mail   31
Chapter 3   The "Cure" May Be the Problem   53
Chapter 4   What the Whistleblowers Have to Say   63
Chapter 5   Indicting Big Pharma   71
Chapter 6   When One Antidepressant Alone
Isn't Enough   77
Chapter 7   Exposing the Betrayal   85
Chapter 8   Politicians, Physicians, and Pharmacists
on the Pharma Payroll   93
Chapter 9   Following the Money   101
Chapter 10 Boys Who Grow Breasts   109

Chapter 11 Risperdal, Prolactin, and the
            Downstream Effects   119
Chapter 12 Band-Aids, Baby Shampoo, and Big Pharma   135

            Afterword Don't Trust a Felon   149
            Acknowledgments   165
            About Sidney D. Kirkpatrick   169
            Notes   171

Introduction
Death by Prescription

ON APRIL 16, 2009, SEVEN-YEAR-OLD Gabriel Myers locked himself in the bathroom of his suburban Florida foster home, coiled a detachable shower hose around his neck, and hung himself. A bright, charming, and often-sweet little boy with close-cropped blond hair and brown eyes, Gabriel was acting out, his behavior having spiraled out of control over the previous year. The police investigation would reveal a tragedy nearly beyond belief: child service caseworkers were medicating him with adult doses of antipsychotic drugs, the negative side effects of which include an increased risk of suicide and violent behavior.

Prescription drug therapy for young Gabriel hadn't begun in Florida but back in Ohio, where he was living with his grandparents while his mother, Candace, was serving jail time. Gabriel, four years old at the time, had begun wetting his bed and acting out in the classroom. On the recommendation of a school therapist, he was diagnosed with ADHD and put on Adderall XR, an amphetamine that is popularly prescribed to children and teens to enhance concentration in the classroom. The drug may have temporarily masked the symptoms he was being treated for, but the root cause of his misbehavior wasn't something chemical stimulants could remedy. It rarely is. Gabriel had repeatedly been molested at knifepoint by a twelve-year-old schoolmate. An abuse report was filed two years after the sexual abuse occurred, but no follow-up was conducted. By the time state authorities were made aware of Gabriel's molestation, he was living with his mother in Florida.[i]

Gabriel came to the attention of police in 2008, when Broward County patrolmen found his mother, Candace, unconscious in her car parked behind a Denny's restaurant. In the front seat beside her, they found powder and crack cocaine along with Xanax and oxycodone in unmarked pharmaceutical containers. Gabriel, then age six, was in the backseat. The Florida Department of Children and Families (DCF) took custody of Gabriel pending legal proceedings against his mother. Gabriel's father, Rocky Newman, was unable to assume custody because he was serving time in a Florida prison. For the next eleven months, Gabriel would be a ward of the state.[ii]

During his initial DCF evaluation, Gabriel was forthcoming about his mother's drug addiction and the molestation he had suffered in Ohio. He was again diagnosed with ADHD and was this time placed on the next-generation amphetamine Vyvanse. Though it was only approved for use by adults, Vyvanse could, like the vast majority of drugs used to treat ADD and ADHD, be prescribed to a child "off-label" with a physician's approval. "Off-label" means that even though the FDA has not approved the drug for a specific condition, doctors can prescribe it if they think it is the best option.

However, rather than enhancing Gabriel's ability to behave in the classroom, Gabriel became more agitated and disruptive. His foster parents and schoolteachers reported more extreme behavioral outbursts; he was inappropriately touching other students and squirted classmates with red dye from a spray bottle. Gabriel was prescribed a combination of Lexapro, used to treat anxiety disorders in teens and adults, and Zyprexa, an antipsychotic that was approved by the FDA for adults with schizophrenia. Both of these drugs are known to increase the risk of violence and suicide. Patients sometimes suffer sudden mood swings and an inability to control rage. His court-appointed psychiatrist apparently didn't know or take the trouble to investigate.

In the last few days of his life, Gabriel told classmates that he felt a strong desire to kill people but didn't have a plan in mind. His teachers reported that he sometimes appeared dazed in class and would trip, fall, or walk into things. At other times, he would suddenly laugh or cry uncontrollably. His medication was changed once more, this time to Symbyax, a powerful Zyprexa compound mixed with Prozac. He was also informed by DCF caseworkers that his mother would no longer have visitation rights and that he would be relocated to Ohio, where the alleged molestation had occurred.

On the day before he took his own life, Gabriel complained of severe stomach problems, was lightheaded and nauseous, and vomited in the school lunchroom. He was excused from classes and didn't return to school the next day. Though state law mandated that he be supervised by a foster parent or certified caregiver, he was home alone with his foster father's nineteen-year-old son, who was not trained or equipped to handle an emergency situation. At lunchtime, Gabriel tossed the meal that had been prepared for him into the kitchen trash can, announced that he was going to take his own life, and locked himself in the bathroom.

Responsibility for Gabriel's suicide can reasonably be shared by many, foremost among them his own parents, who were clearly unable to care for their son. However, there were many opportunities for intervention by those who were charged with protecting him. Had police investigated Gabriel's sexual-abuse claims in a more timely way, he might have been put under the supervision of a therapist who was specifically trained to address his particular needs. A subsequent investigation substantiated Gabriel's story but not in time to do the most good or save other children from a teenage sexual predator at large in an Ohio elementary school. Florida authorities also didn't request a copy of his child welfare history in Ohio, which would have presumably helped caseworkers and teachers better understand why the child felt compelled to act out.

Most troubling of all was how Gabriel had been medicated for the last year of his life. Rather than deal with the root cause of his behavior, his DCF-appointed psychiatrist medicated him with powerful psychotropic drugs used to sedate adult patients. As the police investigation revealed, Gabriel's court-appointed psychiatrist spent no more than a few minutes with the boy before prescribing him these medications and, when later questioned by reporters, said that he could not specifically recall Gabriel as he was one of many foster children in his care. Lack of a proper interview, however, did not prevent the psychiatrist from writing prescriptions that increased the likelihood of violent behavior. Moreover, permission to administer these drugs was not obtained from Gabriel's mother or the courts, as mandated by state law. The only document on record was a generic medical release signed by Candace on the night police found her unconscious from a drug overdose.[iii]

Although it is abundantly clear that Gabriel fell between the cracks and didn't get the help he clearly needed, the sad truth is that his story is not uncommon. Twenty million children in the United States today are diagnosed with mental disorders that psychiatrists prescribe antipsychotic drugs for. The checklist of behaviors these children suffer from—highlighted on drug-company-sponsored parent questionnaires found on the Internet or in literature in pediatric waiting rooms—can be as minor as "losing too many pencils," "does not listen to his teachers," "can't sit still in his chair," and "runs about or climbs excessively at inappropriate times." What was once considered normal child and adolescent behavior has now become a condition drugs are recommended for in one-third of all pediatric psychiatrist evaluations. These drugs expose children to side effects that can be far worse than the condition for which they are prescribed. Among these side effects are Parkinson's-like symptoms, extreme weight gain, diabetes, female-like breast growth in men and boys, psychosis, suicide, and a condition that's sometimes referred to as an "urge to kill."

Let us not forget the murder of twelve students and a teacher and the wounding of twenty-six others at Columbine High School. At least one, and possibly both, of the two shooters was being medicated with psychiatric drugs.[iv] More recently, there was the case of Aaron Alexis, whose murderous rampage at the Washington Navy Yard left twelve dead. The psychiatric medication he was being given came with an equally dire list of potential side effects, which include mania, paranoia, psychosis, hallucinations, and self-destructive behavior.

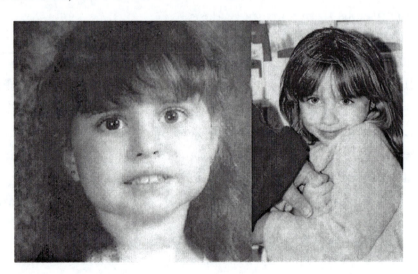

Three years before Gabriel Myers took his own life, four-year-old ADD-diagnosed Rebecca Riley died of a drug overdose of the antipsychotics Seroquel and Depakote. Rebecca's teachers reported that she appeared to be so medicated that she had to be helped walking up the stairs and sitting in her chair at preschool. Three months after Gabriel's death, toddler Destiny Hager died from taking Seroquel, Geodon, and Risperdal among other powerful adult antipsychotics prescribed to children with ADD and ADHD. Her psychiatrist had also placed six other youngsters on antipsychotics, including one two-year-old, two three-year-olds, and a four-year-old.[v] And these are merely the cases that make the headlines. The vast majority of children's deaths from psychiatric drugs go unreported. I hear about them because the families of victims visit my law office and tell me their stories, wanting my help and counsel.

The tragedy is that I know the deaths of these children could have been prevented. Five years before Gabriel's suicide, I filed multiple lawsuits aimed at keeping these drugs from being prescribed to children. My litigation resulted in our firm winning the largest settlement ever paid by one defendant, Eli Lilly, for its marketing of Zyprexa. In presenting our case, I submitted overwhelming documentary evidence and sworn testimony describing how Lilly had knowingly manipulated test results that were presented to the US Food and Drug Administration (FDA) and had assembled dedicated sales teams to illegally sell Zyprexa to children. Within a fifteen-month period, I had also successfully won record-breaking settlements against AstraZeneca for its illicit sales of Seroquel and against Pfizer for its marketing of Geodon and other drugs. I would subsequently win another record-breaking settlement from Johnson & Johnson over its marketing campaigns for Risperdal and Invega.

These pharmaceutical giants had spent billions of dollars illegally targeting their sales campaigns at patients their drugs were not approved for and for whom there was no medical evidence that they were effective. Kickbacks and other incentives had been paid to physicians, most notably to child psychiatrists, in particular to those caring for foster children. Pharmaceutical company marketing departments, not independent and impartial researchers, wrote reviews of these drugs for the major medical journals. And making matters worse, our regulatory agencies contributed to the deceit. As former FDA scientist Leo Lutwak has said, "If the American people knew some of the things that went on at the FDA, they'd never take anything but Bayer aspirin."[vi]

The sad truth is that my litigation didn't save the life of Gabriel Myers. Eli Lilly paid out an enormous sum to settle the case, and for a few months, the company closed lower on the New York Stock Exchange. Investors, not corporate executives, paid the price. Also, for a time, the negative side effects of Zyprexa and its marketing to children made front page news. The same was true of our settlements with AstraZeneca, Pfizer, and Johnson & Johnson. Yet despite the landmark multibillion-dollar payout to US taxpayers and to patients who had been harmed, no corporate decision makers went to jail. Nor did these companies have to publicly reveal what they had done. The vast majority of documents we submitted to the courts were, by judicial order, never made public.

Today, all of these drugs—Zyprexa, Seroquel, Geodon, Risperdal, and Invega along with newer and dangerous antipsychotics such as Abilify—are still on the market and are routinely prescribed to children who are, in my opinion, too young to legitimately be diagnosed as suffering from the psychotic disorders these drugs have been approved for. Test results of these drugs' side effects are routinely deemed to be proprietary information and hence are not available to consumers, US government prosecutors, or even the FDA, the institution charged with regulating these drugs. The US Congress failed to ratify legislation that would have called for increased drug monitoring and closer supervision of children in foster care and other publicly funded programs on the grounds that doing so would place undue burden on the pharmaceutical industry—never mind seven-year-old Gabriel Myers, four-year-old Rebecca Riley, or toddler Destiny Hager.

In the legal climate we live in, a corporation's right to free speech, even when it's proven to be lies, often trumps the rights of consumers. Just ask our current Supreme Court.

The courts and our governmental regulators delivered a clear message: even though the pharmaceutical companies illegally marketed their antipsychotics and knowingly withheld drug studies that might have reasonably resulted in their removal from pharmacy shelves, the government declared that these companies could, after all, go ahead and sell them to children. Apparently, the taxpayer-funded psychiatrist who had prescribed them to Gabriel Myers also wasn't at fault, which is why today he not only still has his medical license, but also has a thriving practice treating foster children.[vii]

If this sounds unfair, it's because it is. If this doesn't make common sense, it's because it doesn't. It's the reality where we, as a nation, have found ourselves. Betrayals of the public trust have become so commonplace that the vast majority of us have begun taking injustice for granted. We accept lies even when we know we are being lied to. We accept the empty promises of reform with deep-seated cynicism and believe we are powerless to do anything about it.

But it doesn't have to be this way.

Rather than throwing up our hands in resignation or taking to the streets in angry and unfocused protest, it's possible to direct our outrage in ways that can and do make a difference. I know because I've succeeded in doing this in the courtroom—not to the extent or as effectively as I would have liked but long enough to know that justice can and will ultimately triumph when the truth is exposed. As I have sought to convey in these pages, fighting for justice demands a willingness to carefully examine the facts, think clearly about the nature of the betrayal, understand what can be done about it, and find a solution that will do the most good. Democracy is not a spectator sport. The powerful corporate and government forces that minimize the less powerful must be challenged, even in the face of overwhelming odds. This is why I'm writing this book and why I'm back in court fighting on behalf of Gabriel Myers and thousands of children like him.

I'll not rest until I've exposed the truth. Nor should you.

CHAPTER 1

Bush v. Gore: How the Fox Got in the Henhouse

IN MY NEARLY FIVE DECADES practicing law, I have litigated some of our nation's most loathsome betrayals of public trust: from birth defects caused by a drug purportedly designed to help pregnant women, deadly diet pills, FDA-approved vaccines that are actually poisonous, and legislative and judicially-created preemption laws protecting corporate criminals from prosecution and responsibility. But it was voter fraud litigation I filed in the 2000 presidential election that gave me an insider's look at what has turned out to be the greatest betrayal of all. Had voting rights protections in Florida been enforced and justice served in our Supreme Court, there might never have been an Iraq War, the mortgage crisis melt-down, our trillion-dollar deficit, a polarized and ineffective Congress, or a pharmaceutical industry that today operates like a crime syndicate.

I understand the skepticism you may have in my making such a bold pronouncement. Hindsight, as they say, can take you only so far. But please indulge me while I explain the voter fraud that took place in Florida in 2000 and how this travesty of justice left a fox guarding our executive henhouse. Though you may not agree with the conclusions I have drawn, you will gain an insight into how I practice law and, in the chapters ahead, understand the many reasons I feel compelled to try and rein in a pharmaceutical industry that's out of control. It's not that I'm less offended by other corporate misdeeds, injustices, and influence peddling. Rather, I believe it's my calling to serve children, the infirm, and the elderly—those whom the pharmaceutical industry invariably chooses to exploit and who, like Gabriel Meyers, most often fall through the cracks when our nation fails.

Like so many of my cases that start out as issues affecting my friends, my family, and our coworkers and gradually spread into the larger community, my voter fraud investigation was triggered by a telephone call, in this case from my mother-in-law,

Bobbie Mitnik, in Palm Beach County. She phoned my office in Philadelphia on Election Day afternoon, November 7, 2000, to express her deep concern. She had entered her polling place intending to vote Democrat but found the ballot on the punch card vote recorder at her polling station to be so confusing that she couldn't be certain if she had voted for Democrat Al Gore or ultra-conservative Reform Party candidate Pat Buchanan. Not only that, but according to her, the pre-election instruction booklet she received in the mail, which contained the sample ballot she had filled out at home, was laid out differently than the one displayed on her Votomatic vote recorder in the polling booth.

Upset, Bobbie asked me what could be done. After calming her down and promising that I would look into it, I phoned friends and other family in Palm Beach and discovered that her experience that Tuesday was not unique. Other elderly Floridians in that county had encountered the same problem.

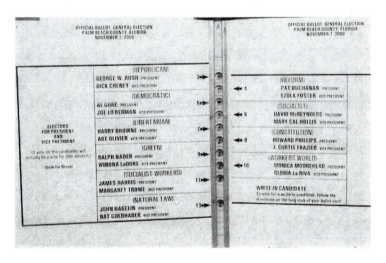

The infamous "butterfly ballot," as it was later known, hadn't listed the three presidential candidates' names one atop the other on a single page as had been done elsewhere in Florida but, instead, had put Gore's and Buchanan's names on different pages opposite one another, making it difficult for the voter to know where they should punch the card for the candidate of their choice. Al Gore's was the second name on the first page of the ballot, just beneath George W. Bush, but to vote for Gore, one had to punch the third hole in a line down the middle of the two pages. Voters were punching the second hole on the left thinking it was for Gore, but the vote was cast for Buchanan, whose name was listed first on the second page.

The informal phone queries I conducted from Philadelphia revealed what the press would announce the next morning: like my mother-in-law, hundreds and perhaps thousands of voters were confused. Complaints to the Palm Beach election supervisors were so numerous that the telephone lines were jammed the entire day of the election. Moreover, I had only to compare the tabulated vote favoring Bush with the exit polls returns favoring Gore to see a glaring inconsistency. Something wasn't right in sunny Palm Beach.

I can be accused of many things, but sitting on my hands is not one of them. First on my agenda was calling my friend Ed Rendell, the former Philadelphia mayor, future governor of Pennsylvania, and at that time the chair of the Democratic National Committee. Rendell agreed I should "get down there, figure it out, and see what could be done." On my own dime, of course.

Forty-eight hours later, Florida friends and colleagues Dave Krathen and Gary Farmer joined me at the Palm Beach County Courthouse to file a class action suit seeking to enjoin the certification of the Palm Beach County vote by Katherine Harris, the Republican Secretary of State. We couldn't have imagined that what began with my mother-in-law's telephone call would mushroom into multiple state and federal complaints that would ultimately result in a post election battle in the US Supreme Court. But that's the exciting thing about what I do and what I believe all of us must do to protect our rights as citizens: voice a complaint. We don't have to see the larger picture to set the wheels in motion. Merely taking the first step will often trigger events well beyond our imagination.

Most of those forty-eight hours leading up to our Palm Beach filing were spent in transit, racing from one place to another, collecting ballots and other documentary materials, gathering voters' affidavits, and assembling the help we needed to draft the complaint. To our delight, Judge Kathleen Kroll granted our restraining order that Thursday afternoon and scheduled a formal hearing before Judge Lucy Chernow Brown to take place five days later on Tuesday, November 14, at 1:00 p.m.

I alerted Ed Rendell of our filing and requested as much legal help and assistance as he could provide. He embraced our efforts, as neither the Al Gore campaign nor the Democratic Party had yet mobilized to challenge the election. Rendell put me in touch with campaign volunteers and fellow Philadelphia attorneys who were familiar with post-election litigation. The result was *Rogers and Kaplan v. Palm Beach Canvassing Commission.*

As it turned out, we were in an important position at the head of a long line of other soon-to-be-filed litigation challenging the Palm Beach vote. In addition to the controversial ballot layout, which had possibly been designed to mislead voters into casting their ballots for candidates not of their choosing, serious other questions were being raised. Many thousands of votes hadn't been counted because the pointer or stylus used in the Votomatic punch-card machine hadn't cleanly penetrated the ballot. If a hole in the ballot card was not cleanly punched through, leaving the much-discussed "hanging" or "dimpled chads," the tabulating machines didn't count the vote.

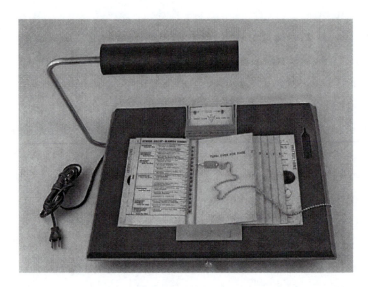

The problem was that Votomatic machines in black-majority precincts were three times more likely to leave hanging or dimpled chats than in nonblack precincts. Had inferior Votomatic machines been installed in precincts where the Democratic vote was expected to be higher than the Republican vote?

Another controversial subject that Gary and I would bring to public attention was the paper stock the ballots were printed on. The stock delivered to the various polling sites was not uniform throughout the state. The thicker the paper stock, the more likely it was that the stylus wouldn't punch a hole cleanly through it. As the Florida ballots were manufactured in the Dallas suburb of Addison, Texas, the home state of Republican candidate George W. Bush, you have to wonder. Were poor-quality punch cards sent to polling stations where Gore was expected to do well and higher-quality punch cards sent elsewhere?

These and so many other issues would require us to conduct extensive research. In the meantime, however, in preparation for our November 14 hearing, we wrote bench memos on the relevant legal issues, most particularly why the butterfly ballot did not meet the requirements of Florida's election code. To buttress our case, we called expert statisticians who would present the court with data that conclusively showed that the Palm Beach County ballot's layout resulted in two thousand or more votes intended for Al Gore that were instead cast for Pat Buchanan. This was, incidentally, just what Buchanan was telling the media. He too had been astonished by the number of votes for him in Palm Beach, a county where he had not campaigned and had virtually no support. A vote for him, Buchanan readily admitted, reflected votes intended for

Gore. Miscast votes, however, were not the only problem. As the *Miami Herald* would later confirm, voters in Palm Beach County were one hundred times more likely than elsewhere in South Florida to invalidate their ballots by voting for both Gore and Buchanan.[viii]

Theresa LaPore, the Palm Beach election supervisor who approved and helped to design the butterfly ballot, was helpful to our cause. Before her abrupt refusal to publicly discuss the matter, she granted an interview to local media acknowledging that the ballot design had been laid out substantively differently than in other counties. Her intention, she said, was to increase the font size on the ballot card, so it could be read more easily by the elderly residents of Palm Beach, but the effect turned out to be confusing. "Madame Butterfly," as LaPore came to be known, regretted her candid remarks, as they confirmed our underlying belief that Palm Beach voters were treated differently than in other counties and in the country at large.

Further suspicion was cast on the ballot design when an investigation revealed that a similar design by LaPore's predecessor had been equally problematic. As the *Palm Beach Post* would report, a butterfly ballot four years earlier had caused an estimated fourteen thousand votes intended for Republican Bob Dole to be dismissed for double punching. Dole was the second name on the 1996 ballot, just as Al Gore was in 2000. Rather than redesigning the ballot and replacing the equipment, the same machines and ballot type had been used again. More significantly, this information had been concealed from voters in 1996 and was again in 2000.[ix]

Later revelations would cast even more doubt on the reliability of the voting machines. The ones used in Palm Beach were not authentic Votomatics but antiquated, imitation, or "clone" Votomatics produced by the Data-Punch Corporation in Illinois. As the *Miami Herald* would report, LaPore's twenty-year-old machines were peppered with worn-out, outdated, and ineffective parts, which included inflexible and cracked plastic springs, battered templates, and worn rubber T-strips. *Herald* reporter David Kidwell, aware of the machine's faults, visited the warehouse where they were stored and ran his own tests on them. His test ballots showed a significant number of dimpled chads, imperfections that would be rejected by computer scanners when counting votes.

If this were not reason enough to demand a recount, in predominantly black and Democratic Duval County, a dot mysteriously showed up on computer scanning machines, causing the counting device to see it as a vote. When the dot was coupled with a vote for another candidate, which was almost always Gore, the machine saw two votes and counted neither, leading to a loss of about three thousand votes for Gore. Over- or undercounting also took place in districts that used ballots on which the voter filled in the oblong area next to the chosen candidate with a provided pencil, but, in these instances, the voter's intent was usually clear.

Allegations of fraud and misconduct continued unabated. As the *Miami Herald* reported, LaPore's poll workers had learned of serious mechanical problems even before the polls opened but had done nothing to correct them. By state law, poll workers are required to confirm the accuracy of ballot books on all machines immediately before precincts open. This includes testing all machines. The machines in Palm Beach County and some in Miami-Dade County failed those mechanical tests but remained in service anyway.[x] There was, as our statistical analysis showed, an incontrovertible correlation between these faulty tests conducted by poll workers before 7:00 a.m. and the precincts that reported high numbers of rejected votes later in the day.

Had a criminally inclined element in Florida learned from the mistakes made four years earlier and used them to their advantage in the 2000 election? I didn't yet know the full extent of the behind-the-scenes decisions that contributed to the faulty Palm Beach vote, but I suspected that we were onto something.

What we were up against became clear the day before our court appearance, when Dave Krathen and I met in Gary Farmer's office in Fort Lauderdale and were dismayed to discover that Bush campaign attorneys had filed a half-dozen motions to stop our having the hearing before the specifics of our case became known. To my consternation, Bush's people had hired the Greenberg Traurig law firm based in Miami, a formidable foe with hundreds of attorneys on staff. Incidentally, the firm's founding partner and CEO was Larry Hoffman, my first cousin by marriage. This was now a family battle, and I dug my heels in.

First, we had to move our litigation forward while still keeping it from being transferred to another, and perhaps less accommodating, court. Second, because the Democratic Party had now jumped into the fray by demanding a manual recount in Palm Beach County, we had to be prepared to argue a range of issues well beyond the confusion stemming from the faulty ballot. More than anything else, we had to educate the public about what had taken place.

The challenges of doing so in such a short time frame were daunting, and our opposition had all the advantages. George W. Bush, brother of the governor of Florida, Jeb Bush, had technically already won the election, and Katherine Harris, the Secretary of State of the Commonwealth of Florida, was co-chair of Bush's Florida election committee. Harris had the power to declare that the mandatory recount already underway be stopped, a power she executed the following Monday morning in Palm Beach County, as she had already done in Broward, Miami-Dade, and Volusia Counties. At that moment more than ever, the public needed to be told not only what our legal team was doing but why.

By the afternoon of our November 14 appearance, the press was reporting allegations of electoral fraud throughout the state. Improper ballot design and defective equipment combined to create a flawed election, and a flawed election was what Palm Beach got. The effect was to make Palm Beach, where the first court hearing was to take place, ground zero in the post-election controversy.

It is difficult to describe the sea of people who descended upon what was otherwise a sleepy Florida courthouse, where attorneys, judges, and police all knew one another, and the only serious outside interference came from the hurricanes that blew in off the Atlantic. A hurricane had arrived that day too, but it wasn't the kind that a meteorologist could have predicted.

Thousands of protesters, mostly African Americans, angry because so many of their votes hadn't been counted, had descended upon Palm Beach. The largest contingent of protesters, led by Reverend Jesse Jackson, marched in the streets and camped out in front of the courthouse, calling, as we did, for the vote recount to be resumed and for a full-fledged nonpartisan inquiry into the butterfly ballots. Standing in opposition to them were Confederate-flag wavers and self-proclaimed neo-Nazis. Claiming their places on the sidelines were hundreds of "volunteer" attorneys in Brooks Brothers suits, state police and sheriffs in riot gear, and television and print reporters from as far away as Los Angeles and Tokyo. Newscasters hovered overhead in helicopters, and their vans blocked the streets.

I felt a mix of emotions: a tremendous desire to remain steadfast in my commitment to represent my mother-in-law and so many more thousands of disenfranchised Florida voters, and trepidation that a race riot would overshadow what we sought to accomplish in court. Most of all, I felt a deep concern for our nation and its leadership.

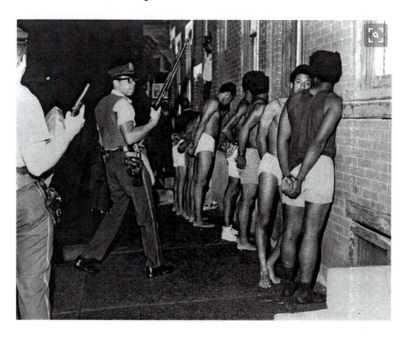

Years earlier, amid race riots outside the Philadelphia courthouse, I had defended the Black Panthers on trumped-up murder and conspiracy charges. I had joined protest marches and demonstrations with the Congress of Racial Equality (CORE) while leading the court battle for higher wages, healthy working conditions, and gender equality on behalf of black janitorial trade unions and maids. Thanks to suits that I brought on behalf of the American Civil Liberties Union (ACLU), we won the rights for young people to vote in the ward where they went to college if it differed from their home residences, and drafted inclusive new rules that were used to determine the selection of delegates for presidential conventions.

I don't mention these things to beat my own drum or display my left-leaning liberal roots, but to put our greater national struggle into historical perspective. The sense of anger and betrayal that I felt in Palm Beach was made the more acute because I, a Jew from Brooklyn, and so many others of my generation—whites and blacks and Jews and Gentiles—had fought this battle before. Civil and voter rights legislation was our generation's legacy. There I was, nearly forty-years later, fighting to reclaim lost ground.

I wouldn't get to fire the opening salvo of that battle, however, if I couldn't reach the courthouse. There were so many protesters, police, television crews, and attorneys that we had difficulty reaching the front steps. When our team finally arrived at the front doors, we found them locked by security guards fighting to keep the protest outside. Luckily, I saw a law clerk making his way toward a side entrance, and our team managed to slip in behind him.

I was dumbfounded by what came next. After our hearing was called to order, one judge after another recused her- or himself from hearing our case. No one, it seemed, wanted to jeopardize his career by trying such a high-profile and politically charged litigation—so much for our courageous justices.

Despondent, we left the courthouse fearing the worst. The only positive outcome was an opportunity to file new motions demanding that the election recount be resumed regardless of Katherine Harris's orders. Our argument was simply that the recount from Palm Beach may demonstrate that Gore had actually won the election. If this proved to be the case, there would be no further need to seek the more difficult remedy of staging a new election.

The parade of judges recusing themselves continued the next day until, to our relief, Judge Jorge Labarga took the assignment. As we had anticipated, he deferred judgment on the issues regarding the ballot design, ostensibly because he was not certain the problem could be constitutionally remedied in state court. There was only one day a year set aside for a presidential election, and regardless of how confusing the choice of one ballot over another might be, ordering an election in Palm Beach, and not the entire nation, could be viewed as unconstitutional. That issue would not be decided that day. However, Labarga accepted our argument about the importance of permitting the manual recount to go forward.

Most importantly, Labarga directed the canvassing board to consider any marks on the punch card that clearly showed a voter's intent. In other words, even a punch hole that had not completely removed the chad was deemed eligible to be counted. His order permitting the recount was the first judicial order in Florida of its kind and, needless to say, our *Rogers and Kaplan* case became national and then international news that night. I left the court feeling that we had accomplished a major step forward. I knew ahead of time that the decision would invariably be appealed and the butterfly ballot issues wouldn't necessarily be decided in our favor, but we were well on the way toward establishing the legal framework that could be used to appeal the Florida vote in federal court and, in turn, the results of the 2000 election.

Frustratingly, twenty-seven days later, our case wasn't the one that reached the US Supreme Court. While our Palm Beach litigation came first and was, I believe, the strongest case, the battle over the presidential election had spread into other, much larger counties throughout the state. Eventually, Al Gore's team asked us to withdraw our complaint in favor of another.

My decision to stand down turned out to be the most regrettable of my entire career, for the stakes couldn't have been higher. Knowing in hindsight what we do about the Bush presidency, I should not have left it in the hands of others to fight to uphold our nation's civil rights—protections which I would soon see cast aside in favor of thinly veiled and self-serving corporate interests. I believe that *Rogers and Kaplan* would have been the strongest case to take before the Supreme Court, as it did not rest on politically complicated issues of federal versus states' rights but on consumer fraud. The Palm Beach ballot was improperly designed and the Votomatic machines faulty. Easily proven facts and backed-up science, not ideology or rhetoric, would have ruled the day.

On November 17, three days after our hearing, I had a premonition about what was eventually to be decided by the high court. I took the last flight out of Palm Beach back to Philadelphia that day to attend the celebration of the 150th anniversary of my alma mater, the University of Pennsylvania Law School. The speaker for the festivities was US Supreme Court Justice Sandra Day O'Connor. I found her remarks genuine and inspiring. A tallish woman with white hair and wearing a light-colored dress, she spoke of the heroism and dedication of generations of women who battled a patriarchal system for equality and how, in the years since then, women were entering law schools in ever-increasing numbers and making even greater contributions to the public good. As Justice O'Connor's stirring speech ended, a fire alarm rang, and everyone in the law school auditorium went trooping out of the building with O'Connor aggressively pushing her way to the front of the line to be the first out the door.

The alarm turned out to be false, but the shrill ringing in my ears continued when, on December 12, Justice O'Connor's vote was the deciding one in the ruling that disenfranchised thousands of voters: men and women, young and old, blacks and whites, those who didn't know enough to complain, and those who, like my mother-in-law, did. The court ruled that the state of Florida could not determine the meaning and application of its own laws since to do so would cause "irreparable harm" to petitioner George W. Bush. In other words, the Supreme Court violated the very principles of states' rights that they had themselves set forth on numerous previous occasions. It was a stunning attack on states' rights by a court that had hitherto held the expansion of states' rights as its Holy Grail.

In addition to the victory of federal rights over states' rights, the decision also presented an equally stunning refutation of what had, up until that point, been considered in state and federal courts to be a basic rule concerning conflict of interest: namely, that a judge may not sit on a case in which a family member is party, either as a litigant or an attorney. From that moment onward, judges apparently no longer needed to recuse themselves in such cases. Justice Antonin Scalia participated in the *Bush v. Gore* case and voted in support of Bush even though his lawyer son worked with, and was supervised by, the attorney who represented Bush before the Supreme Court and whom President Bush would subsequently appoint as solicitor general. Scalia himself had been a recent guest at Bush's ranch in Texas. Additionally, Justice Thomas's wife, an attorney and congressional lobbyist, was so intimately involved in the Bush campaign that she was helping draw up a list of possible Bush appointees at more or less the same time her husband was adjudicating on whether Bush would become the next president.[xi]

Even Sandra Day O'Connor, on the eve of the election, displayed her bias when she publicly stated that a Gore victory would be a personal disaster. Her sentiments were echoed by her husband during an election-night party held before the votes had been tabulated, when it was believed that Gore and not Bush had won Florida and, hence, the presidency. He had said that Sandra would have to wait another four years before they could retire to Arizona or else a Democrat would get to appoint her replacement on the Supreme Court.[xii] A Democrat in our nation's highest office simply wouldn't do. Never mind the merits of the case *Bush v. Gore*, which she and the other justices were soon to hear.

When alarm bells rang at the University of Pennsylvania, I didn't know that O'Connor would be the swing vote that would decide the election. My attention was still fixed on Palm Beach, on what could be done about the central problem as I saw it, how faulty machines and their ballots may have been used to favor one candidate over another. To that end, Gary Farmer and I joined another class action suit already underway, this time against the company that had manufactured the Votomatic machines. If we could prove that the machines were inferior and that those who put them into service in Florida knew it, we might find out what had actually happened in Palm Beach on Election Day. At the least, we could gain insight into the identities of the decision makers through discovery and depositions. Florida election officials could easily sidestep the media, but they couldn't ignore a judge's summons to testify under oath.

The class action suit we brought in January 2001 was filed in Illinois against Election Systems & Software (ES&S) and didn't mention the disputed *Bush v. Gore* election. The principal allegation was that their Votomatic system was inherently faulty and produced incorrect counts. The machine and its results were the principal evidence in our favor. Subsidiaries and companies that licensed the machines, such as Data-Punch, were selling products and services necessary for the ongoing use of the Votomatic machines while failing to tell customers that the machines had serious defects that violated consumer fraud statutes. As the machines were used in 29% of the polling places in the 2000 election, we had abundant statistical information upon which to draw. Our team contributed what we had learned in Palm Beach, which could be used to compare and contrast the experience of the Votomatic's usage elsewhere across the nation.

I don't wish to burden you with ever finer details of how I believe voter fraud was engineered in Florida, but as you will see in the chapters to come, the key to understanding the truth of a betrayal is often less a matter of legal reasoning than it is unraveling the tangled knot of the facts of a case. In *Bush v. Gore*, attention must be focused on what election officials knew about the Votomatic machines that were being used to tabulate the vote.

For those fortunate enough not to have cast a ballot by Votomatic, the machine essentially consists of a punch card with a plastic backing that should be replaced when it becomes stiff, although this is rarely the case. The voter slides the card into place over the ballot and uses a stylus to punch out a circle next to the names of the candidates he or she prefers. Theoretically, the punched-out chad lands into the T-strip below which contains chambers to hold the chads corresponding to where they had been on the punch card. There is no way for the voter to know whether or not the chad is in the tray. This is important because if the stylus hasn't detached the chad, there is often no hole for the computer scanner to read when the cards are bundled and run through the counting machine. The vote is then not tabulated.

Our research revealed a variety of reasons why the chad is not removed, creating an "undervote," which means the vote for the intended candidate isn't counted. Made infamous by the Florida election, the hanging chad is a tiny fragment of paper that may literally be hanging by one or two edges. It may sometimes fall off into the tray, in which event the computer scanner counts the hole. Two other types of errant chads are ordinarily never counted. The "pregnant" chad occurs when a hole is poked in the ballot by the tip of the stylus, but remains in place. In the case of the dimpled chad, the stylus merely makes an indentation. Heavy punch card paper, stiff plastic backing, or imprecise positioning of the ballot all contribute to the undervote.

The cards and card stock, however, are not always to blame when the Votomatic fails. In 1968, for example, a flaw in the counting machine in Montana caused Richard Nixon to lose in Republican districts and his Democratic opponent, Hubert Humphrey, to fare poorly in areas where the Democrats were strong. Despite its many faults, which made it less reliable than any other voting method, there are nevertheless times and places where the Votomatic works just fine. Thus, the machine has well-known weaknesses that may or may not present themselves when used.

Although it seems clear that the Votomatic's popularity had a great deal to do with ES&S's legitimate lobbying efforts with officials in both parties, it is a temptation for dishonest politicians and their sponsors because of how easily it can be manipulated to produce false results. If someone, for example, were to use a Votomatic to commit a fraud, it would not be necessary to involve many people. The machine is susceptible to rigging both at the point of origin and at the polling place by using substandard ballot paper that produces chads, or doesn't fit squarely into the Votomatic tray, or using machines that haven't been properly maintained and serviced or have been purposefully misaligned.

Our investigation revealed that this kind of tampering apparently took place in the 1988 election in Florida, in which suspicious results arose in many of the same counties in which fraud was suspected in the 2000 election. In the 1988 affair, Republican Connie Mack and Democrat Buddy Mackay competed for a seat in the U.S. Senate, with Mack defeating Mackay by 34,518 votes out of more than four million cast. In four strong Democratic counties, the Votomatic system recorded 233,000 more votes in the presidential contest than in the senatorial race. If the Votomatic results were to be believed, this would mean that more people in these counties voted for state treasurer and secretary of state than for U.S. senator.

Oddly enough, even the most thorough analysis of *Bush v. Gore* made no mention of *Mackay v. Mack*. The analysis undertaken by *Knight-Ridder* newspapers and *U.S.A. Today* came to the conclusion that Bush won but, on the other hand, Gore had also won. As the report explained, by applying the strictest and most frequently used means of counting, Bush ended up with a lead of 152 votes rather than the official 407. However, if votes that previously hadn't been were counted, voter intent dictated that Gore won by approximately 15,000 votes.

The study laid much blame on the butterfly ballot in Palm Beach County, where Votomatic-type machines were used. Not only had my mother-in-law and I complained about it, but the newspaper researchers did as well. According to them, the alignment of names and punch holes on the cards made it difficult for many voters to figure out how to cast their ballot for Gore and, consequently, they ended up voting for Buchanan or for both of them, creating an overvote in which the machine saw multiple holes for the same office and rejected it. According to the newspaper articles, the election altogether produced 111,000 overvotes. Gore was coupled with another candidate in the overvotes, though not necessarily Buchanan, 76% of the time. The high number of Gore couplings indicated that he was the voter's choice in the large majority of, if not all, such instances.

A further reason to believe that most of the uncounted overvotes had been Gore's, said the study, is that Gore ran 25,000 votes behind the Democratic candidate for senator in the overvote count. In other words, this was the opposite of the Mackay loss, in which he ran astoundingly behind the Democratic candidate for president. To the authors of the *Knight-Ridder* and *U.S.A. Today* study, the discrepancy in the senatorial and presidential votes indicated that chances were good that most people who voted for the Democrat for senator also intended to vote for the Democrat for president. This generalization has merit, but it was not the only or most significant inference to draw. In order for there to be no chicanery in the election, we must believe that the Democratic voters who were too confused to figure out how to vote for president were somehow bright enough to figure out how to vote for U.S. senator, a point which has been ignored in everything I've read on the subject.

It is further apparent that Gore was not only hurt by overvotes, but also by undervotes. This could have happened by providing targeted districts with imperceptibly thicker or more resilient punch card paper, making it more difficult for a stylus to fully penetrate from the top to bottom. Alternately, the paper could have been cut in such a way as to be slightly misaligned at the Gore slot, preventing a chad or partial chad to be released. Regardless of the paper used in the ballot, however, the percentage of overvotes and undervotes was astounding even by Votomatic standards.

I don't pretend to know exactly what happened in Florida, but based on election law expert Gregory Harvey's studies and the *Knight-Ridder/U.S.A. Today* statistical analysis, which has never been refuted, I can see no way in which the results could have come about by chance. Citizens were stripped of their most fundamental right to vote. Worse, their vote would be counted with the evident winners, the Republican Party. With George W. Bush as president, and Jeb Bush, the governor of Florida, W.'s chances for reelection would be significantly enhanced with his party and his older brother in power.

The best place to find the truth about what happened is with Election Systems and Software (ES&S), which was why Gary Farmer and I joined the litigation team bringing the class action suit against them. But as soon as we took up the case, it had to be dropped. The plaintiffs no longer faced being cheated by the suspect Votomatics because the machines were withdrawn before we could litigate the case in court. After the chads went flying in Florida, election officials across the county would no longer touch a Votomatic with a ten-foot stylus. Had the suit actually been litigated, the plaintiff attorneys, including Gary and I, could have questioned ES&S officials about their deal-making with Florida politicians and might have also been able to take depositions from the civil-service and other Floridians who put the Votomatics into service.

We may have to wait years for new evidence to be unearthed by a historian about what happened in Palm Beach in 2000. But as Gary and I have already found by submitting several of the preserved punch cards from Democratic districts to experts, we know that the paper stock, which was not uniform through-out the state, created both over-and under-counting. Were poor quality punch cards sent to polling stations where Gore was expected to do well and higher-quality punch cards sent elsewhere?

I would also call your attention to the immediate aftermath of the 2000 election. To get to its importance, assume, for the moment, that the presidential election in Florida was entirely free of malfeasance on the part of election officials. In that event, Floridian officials would logically be upset at the company whose equipment failures caused the state to suffer national and inter-national embarrassment as they tried to explain how such gross failures could occur on their watch. Significantly, this was not the case, something that should give all voters cause for serious concern.

Floridian officials under Jeb Bush not only failed to launch a proper investigation, but they also bought more ES&S machines. Thanks to lobbyist Sandra Mortham, the former Florida secre-tary of state, twelve Florida counties bought these new voting machines for a total of $70.6 million dollars in taxpayers' money.

The newly purchased ES&S machines arrived loaded with problems, including the mysterious dot that had turned up on some machines in Gore districts in the 2000 election. In the 2002 Democratic primary to choose who would oppose incumbent Jeb Bush for governor, front-runner Janet Reno received an undervote of about 48 percent in heavily Democratic Miami-Dade County. She demanded a recount that was ultimately averted when the election officials inexplicably managed to reconstruct some of the missing votes out of the computer's innards. Reno, not wishing to protract the contest into November, conceded—although like Gore, she had probably won—leaving it up to her lesser-known opponent to unseat Jeb Bush.

He didn't.

The rest, as they say, is history. As a result of the "stolen" 2000 election, I believe our nation was led into two needless wars instead of one warranted police action. Hundreds of thousands of innocents died and torture was legally sanctioned. Our nation became conquerors and invaders, not the liberators of Eisenhower's and MacArthur's times. And in the process, the rich got richer, and the tables tilted further in favor of banks, financiers, and the military industrial complex. Fewer than four hundred families today now possess as many assets as the bottom 150 million, and 95 percent of our nation's economic gains go to the richest 1 percent of Americans.[xiii, xiv] As the average worker is struggling to make ends meet on minimum wage, the owners of our largest corporations are experiencing record-breaking profits, with the CEOs' salaries, stock options, and other benefits five hundred times higher than their average employee.

Had Bush not taken office, we may not have been saddled with draconian Voter ID and redistricting laws that have disenfranchised hundreds of thousands of voters. We also may not have been sold a false bill of goods about the so-called "paper trail" we can use to verify election results—the one in which voters are excluded from actually examining the ballots and where county auditors are not permitted to inspect the proprietary computer software that is used to tabulate the votes.

Under a different chief executive, we might not have a judiciary that increasingly operates on a two-tier system of justice—one for the well off and one for the poor. As has become a veritable cliché in our nation's courts, a defendant with a public defender goes to prison and a defendant with private counsel walks. Most unfair of all, criminals who run companies that steal hundreds of millions of dollars or are responsible for killing or injuring hundreds of thousands of people receive bonuses and promotions, and the thief in the supermarket or the street-corner mugger goes to jail.

With a different chief executive, we may not have had a Supreme Court that decided in favor of Citizen's United, in which corporations have been granted corporate personhood with constitutional rights similar to yours and mine, including that of free speech. That a corporation is not a flesh-and-blood person, can live indefinitely, be bought and sold, headquartered in a foreign country, can amass immense wealth that is not subject to the same taxes as you and me, and whose owners cannot be legally liable for wrongs it commits is beside the point—or so the Supreme Court would have us believe.

This same court applied similarly twisted logic when striking down federal campaign contribution regulations (for the first time in history) by increasing the amount of money donors can contribute to political campaigns. As money constitutes free speech, so our judiciary tells us, why shouldn't corporations be permitted to give freely? Never mind that a dairyman on a small, family-run New Hampshire farm can't compete with the billions that the Monsanto corporation has to spend.

I'll not argue that some or all of these things wouldn't have occurred had Gore, not Bush, sat in the Oval Office, or that Democrats aren't also responsible for many of our nation's travails. But I can tell you with absolute certainty that the 2000 election brought forth a massive tidal wave of corporate influence that infected our government at all levels. Corporate titans, today's equivalent of yesterday's robber barons, were permitted to buy elections, purchase state legislatures, appoint judges, and write laws to benefit themselves. Nowhere is this more evident than with the pharmaceutical industry chieftains, whose lobbyists became key players in the Bush administration, and under whose influence the FDA became the "fast drug approval" agency.

Among the most powerful of those pharmaceutical corporations is Eli Lilly, whom Gary Farmer and I would take to court in the same state where we had earlier filed voter fraud charges, and which was the case that became the genesis of the litigation described in these pages. In retrospect, our choice to team-up and take on Lilly was providential—either that or a recipe for disaster. Not only were members of the Bush family major stockholders in Eli Lilly and other pharmaceutical companies, but they were beholden to the industry in other ways as well.

After leaving his post as CIA director, George H. W. Bush was appointed a director on the Lilly board, an honor bestowed upon him by the wealthy and influential father of future Vice-President Dan Quayle, the owner of a controlling interest in the company. Then, and later, George H.W. Bush would successfully lobby to permit drug companies to sell obsolete or domestically-banned pharmaceuticals to Third World countries. While Vice-President, he would continue to act on behalf of pharmaceutical company interests by personally requesting the IRS to give special tax breaks for Lilly and other drug companies.[xv]

Also serving on Lilly's board of directors was Bush 2000 campaign contributor Ken Lay, the former CEO of Enron, who President George W. Bush and the First Lady joined on an Enron corporate jet on their first trip to Washington after winning the election. All of us know, of course, what happened there: Enron would go on to become the poster-child of institutionalized, systematic and creatively planned accounting fraud, that which would set the stage for the Wall Street subprime mortgage crisis of 2008.

As would soon become evident to Gary and me, the Bush connection to Eli Lilly and the Big Pharma "alumni club" ran much deeper than just this. Mitch Daniels, a former vice president of Lilly, became Bush's director of management and budget. Sidney Taurel, another former Lilly CEO, would join Bush's Homeland Security Advisory Council. Secretary of Defense Donald Rumsfeld served on the board of Eli Lilly partners

Amylin Pharmaceuticals and Gilead Sciences. Similarly, administration veterans would transition easily back and forth to Lilly's senior management. Among them was Alex Azar, who was Bush's deputy secretary of the Department of Health and Human Services, during which he oversaw such agencies as the FDA, the National Institute of Health (NIH), the Center for Disease Control (CDC), and the Centers of Medicare and Medicaid Services. After leaving the Bush administration, Azar would become the senior vice president of corporate affairs and communication for Lilly.

Then there was Big Pharma's shill Dr. Andrew von Eschenback, whom President Bush appointed the head of the National Cancer Institute and who would later be tapped to head the FDA. As the Union of Concerned Scientists and the National Academies of Sciences, Engineering, and Medicine's Institute of Medicine would report in 2006, under Eschenback's tenure, the agency was "perverting science for political and financial benefactors."[xvi]

Care to guess which drug company dominated the lobbying pack? In our new pharmaceutical litigation, Gary and I encountered so many conflicts of interest that our case should have been justifiably called Lillygate.

CHAPTER 2

Your Prozac Is in the Mail

PRIVACY & PROZAC
CNN AMERICAN MORNING   7:09a ET
ES SUN AFTER HE WAS INJURED BY EXPLOSIVE DEVICE

HAD I NOT RECEIVED THAT providential telephone call from my
mother-in-law in Palm Beach, and subsequently teamed-up with
Gary Farmer to file *Bush v. Gore*, I might never have known
about a highly unorthodox 2002 Florida scheme to market a new
Eli Lilly drug, Prozac Weekly—which triggered a tsunami of

pharmaceutical litigation to come. Rather than just advertising Prozac Weekly in the usual ways, and trying to impress upon prescribers the drug's alleged new benefits, free samples were sent directly to potential customers.

The inciting event that first caught our attention was a package that was sent from a Walgreens Pharmacy in Deerfield, Florida. The recipient, who lived nearby, was a fifty-eight-year-old caregiver; I'll call her "S. K." to protect what little privacy she has left. Included in the package were four bright, multicolored capsules, which, as S. K. later said, looked like candy and could have been ingested by her grandchildren had they, not she, opened the unsolicited mailing envelope.

In addition to the capsules, a letter from Holy Cross Medical Group, a subsidiary of Holy Cross Hospital in Fort Lauderdale, was enclosed. S. K. was a patient of one of its doctors, Lise Lambert, who, with three colleagues from the same medical group, had signed the letter. It read:

April 2002

Dear Patient,

We are very excited to be able to offer you a more convenient way to take your antidepressant medication. Prozac Weekly is the exact same medication as Prozac, but with convenient, once-a-week dosing.

For your convenience, enclosed you will find a FREE one-month trial of Prozac Weekly. If you wish to try Prozac

Weekly, stop your daily antidepressant one day before starting Prozac Weekly; then take only Prozac Weekly once a week thereafter.

Congratulations on being one step to full recovery.

If you have any questions or concerns, please call our office at your earliest convenience.

S. K. was mystified and disturbed. She had undergone treatment for depression for a number of years, a condition that she didn't want publicized lest it make employers wary of hiring her. About eight years earlier, she had been given a prescription for Prozac, which she had filled at a Walgreens. However, that was in Massachusetts, and since her move to Florida, she'd had no dealings with the Walgreens in Deerfield.

That she was sent Prozac at all was beyond her comprehension. She'd had a bad reaction to it, so her psychiatrist had put her on an alternative antidepressant. There hadn't been any discussion with Dr. Lambert, whom she hadn't seen for months, about changing her medication, so why would her former physician have Walgreens send her a drug she had reacted poorly to in the past?

Had she not had an unfortunate experience with Prozac, she reflected, she might well have taken the free pills, though the mailing contained no warnings about the many adverse effects or descriptions of medical conditions that made use of Prozac inadvisable. For example, pregnant women taking Prozac and several other selective serotonin reuptake inhibitors (SSRIs) run the serious risk of delivering babies with heart defects, and everyone taking the drug increases his or her risk of suicide. The final sentence inviting "Dear Patient" to call the office if she has questions or concerns could hardly constitute a product warning, especially when immediately preceded by the congratulatory "step to full recovery" sentence.

The more S. K. considered her gift, the more alarmed she became. She had no doubt that others had also received it. The "Dear Patient" salutation indicated that it had not come from her personal physician, nor could she imagine her doctor, or other doctors for that matter, using the word "free" in capital letters, much less the term "congratulations." The whole thing smelled of an advertising promotion for a prescription drug, which meant it had to have been going to many people, some of whom would, like her, react poorly to Prozac but would take the free capsules because they'd assume their doctors would never send them anything that could harm them. She decided to see Gary Farmer in Fort Lauderdale. Gary's expertise was not product liability or class action law, but he knew it was mine. Pharmaceutical company fraud and misbehavior was one of my specialties.

"You aren't going to believe this" was how he began our conversation.

Gary was right. It was stranger than fiction. Here was a drug company bypassing physicians and its own sales reps by taking its mind-altering antidepressants directly to the consumer.

I hadn't yet thought through what laws were being broken, but it was surely beyond the scope of ethical behavior. Not only had S. K.'s personal medical records been somehow made public, but that information was also being used to market prescription medication directly to her in her home by mail no less. This had nothing to do with "treating her condition," as the letter suggested. It had everything to do with generating profits.

Soon thereafter, we received a call from a woman whose sixteen-year-old son received Prozac extended release in the mail. He had never been prescribed the drug. Were we looking at a tsunami of prescription drugs being sent unsolicited by one of the largest drug manufacturers in the country?

As Gary and I soon learned, there had already been much litigation over Prozac, and nearly all of it centered on the drug's negative side effects. Most notable was a case in Kentucky that didn't get much media attention but spoke volumes about the minefield we were about to walk into.

The case involved a forty-seven-year-old printer who, one month after he began taking Prozac, opened fire at his workplace with his AK-47. The surviving victims of the slaughter had sued Lilly, claiming that an adverse reaction to Prozac had pushed the shooter over the edge. Among the revelations to emerge during the trial were previously undisclosed clinical tests linking Prozac users to sudden and extreme violence.[xvii] These tests had apparently not been submitted to the FDA during the drug approval process. Or had they? As it was also revealed at this trial, five of the nine FDA scientists charged with investigating Prozac were on Big Pharma's payroll, and two had actually conducted Prozac clinical trials for Lilly. And even these revelations couldn't compare to what the presiding judge would discover after the case was settled in Lilly's favor.

Similar to the surprise ending in a John Grisham novel, the judge discovered that Lilly had cut a secret deal with the plaintiff attorneys not to introduce corporate business records, drug trial results, and company correspondence into the public record.[xviii] Lilly would ultimately have to pay a penalty for collusion with opposing counsel, but unfortunately for those who took Lilly's drugs, the company was not forced to make public the documents it had gone to such lengths to keep out of the court record.

Perhaps Gary and I could somehow make public whatever Lilly had to hide in our new case. As I've said and will repeat again, big things can come out of small first steps.

Based on what I've written so far, you might say that I don't think very highly of pharmaceutical industry practices and that I have serious reservations about the FDA's ability to regulate it. You would be right. This doesn't mean, however, that I don't understand the miracle of modern science or appreciate the contributions that the industry has brought to the world. HIV has gone from a death sentence to a chronic disease. Heart bypasses and the drugs that make them possible have saved the lives of many of my friends. My problem begins when marketers, not scientists, become the decision makers, and dollars and cents trump health concerns. And this case, with its direct-to-the-consumer marketing of drugs, seemed to be the epitome of all that was wrong with the industry.

Based on what we were learning, Gary and I filed a class action in Florida state court with S. K. and others as plaintiffs. The defendants were Walgreens, the hospital, its group practice, and its practitioners, along with Indianapolis-based Eli Lilly.

Our lawsuit made news not only in Fort Lauderdale but was also picked up by the Associated Press and the *Wall Street Journal*. It also hit the front page of the *New York Times*[xix], where I was quoted as saying, "What they should be doing is developing a drug to diminish their greed."

I used the same or similar response when the electronic media came calling. S. K. and I were interviewed on ABC's *Good Morning America*, on CBS's *Early Show*, on CNN, and on National Public Radio. It struck me that the media's strong reaction was largely based on shock: until then, it had just never occurred to most people that a drugstore would mail free samples of a prescription drug, let alone one as powerful and addictive as Prozac. Doctors often give out samples, but when they do, they are there to discuss the medication with the patient, and the medication itself is accompanied by the required warnings.

Following the onslaught of bad publicity created by the suit, the defendants dove for cover. Holy Cross Hospital, its medical group, and the medical group's staff took refuge in silence. Walgreens claimed it had been given prescriptions for the samples and certainly never would have mailed them if it hadn't. Moreover, the company had received coupons from Eli Lilly to be submitted for reimbursement. If anyone was to blame, it was Eli Lilly, or so the rationale went.

Lilly, in turn, faulted four overzealous pharmaceutical reps for coming up with the entire marketing scheme and presumably for paying for the printing and the free Prozac mailing out of their own pockets. They were subsequently fired and sued Lilly for wrongful termination, claiming they were just doing what they were told. Even if it had been their idea, it is hard to understand why Lilly would be upset with them, as it's been maintaining since our suit was filed that the mailings signed by physicians were "well intentioned and perfectly appropriate conduct."

For a period of at least seven months prior to the day S. K. got her free gift, other patients had also received a free prescription for Prozac Weekly. Among them was sixteen-year-old M. G., who came home from school to discover his free package of Prozac Weekly. The prescription was sent with a letter from the head doctor of the family practice that he and his mother went to in West Palm Beach. M. G. was confused. He was not taking an antidepressant and never had. He said he had "no clue" where the sender would get the idea that he wanted or needed Prozac. Then there was fifty-nine-year-old A. P., who lived thirty miles away in Fort Lauderdale. She received a similar package to M. G.'s from her doctor. "At first I was startled and confused," she said. "Why would they suggest I take Prozac Weekly?"

A. P. didn't realize she was targeted because she took Zoloft, a drug manufactured by one of Lilly's competitors. She had been taking it for panic attacks she suffered as a result of the September 11 terrorist attacks. She didn't think anyone besides her physician knew she suffered from panic attacks and was concerned that this had somehow become public. She said she threw the pills in the garbage disposal and shredded the package. A third woman, J. N., had been taking Prozac but had stopped several years earlier. As she had just applied for life insurance, quite correctly stating that she was not currently being treated for any psychiatric condition, she became fearful the insurer would reject her if it discovered the apparently readily available false information about her.

We didn't know and ultimately never found out exactly how extensive the free Prozac Weekly effort was. However, Gary and I have evidence of its taking place in California, Oregon, and possibly Washington, and there is also some reason to believe it was practiced in other places nationwide. According to an Oregon pharmaceutical rep who quit Lilly because of his misgivings about the program, Lilly's regional sales managers were putting heavy pressure on the reps to increase sales of Prozac Weekly beginning in the latter part of 2001 and, as far as we knew, were continuing the campaign. Its ostensible purpose in developing the new weekly formula, it seems, had less to do with convenience for the patient and more to do with extending its patent rights and maintaining Prozac's share of the booming antidepressant market.

The market was about to be inundated by lower-priced generic tablets, and Lilly was expected to lose about 80 percent of its $2.5 billion annual Prozac revenue and needed a financial lift. If Lilly could get its Prozac customers to switch to Prozac Weekly, which was under patent, the problem would be solved.

The drug company's plan was for the drug reps to go to doctors with whom they had good relations and from whom they'd receive the names of patients on Prozac and other antidepressants. The reps would then go to a cooperative pharmacist who would fill the prescriptions and receive reimbursement coupons from Lilly for their costs. The Prozac Weekly tablets would then be returned to the doctors in the patients' names to be distributed the next time the patient came in. If the patient didn't want the Prozac Weekly, the doctor could simply block out that patient's name and fill in another. Sometimes the reps would double up by getting a second Lilly reimbursement coupon to be used for the same patient. It's unclear exactly what doctors gained by participating, but there is indication of Lilly's largesse toward them in the form of perks and promotional incentives—a subject I would repeatedly encounter in my litigation to come.

The drug reps would get bonuses from Lilly for their performance, and wherever this scheme was carried out, Lilly showed huge spikes in sales of Prozac Weekly, for which it was paying both the cost of the prescriptions to pharmacies and the bonuses to reps. The Oregon drug rep who quit did so because he believed the scheme was in violation of Lilly's own authorized policies and procedures. He raised the same ethical considerations we described in our lawsuit. This drug rep also believed this marketing scheme may have endangered the health of some patients who were switched from another antidepressant to Prozac in apparent violation of FDA rules.

The rep informed his superiors about what he viewed as Lilly's illicit or illegal practices shortly after he learned of the marketing program in late 2001. The practice was allegedly stopped but resumed several months later. When the rep continued to complain, he was told he was not being a team player, which lead to his resignation. His narrative, the important points of which are backed up by at least one other Lilly drug rep in Oregon, made it appear that the marketing scheme originated at a regional level and didn't necessarily have the approval of Lilly's corporate headquarters. However, Lilly's corporate headquarters had to be aware of large increases in "sales" of Prozac Weekly in some areas but not in others.

In the districts where sales were greatest, as its records would have shown, Lilly was not receiving income but was paying out an amount that was commensurate with its increased sales. Either Lilly was incomprehensibly negligent in its oversight of its own employees, or it encouraged the plan because it would show, no matter how falsely, sales growth that would have a positive effect on the company's stock

Lilly may, in fact, have seen its conduct as appropriate. Long before we came along and the revelations of the Kentucky trial, Lilly and its competitors in the pharmaceutical industry had been deeply involved in manipulating patients' welfare to add to their profits. They had paid pharmacies, benefits managers, and doctors in the hopes of switching their patients from a competitor's brand to theirs. Two other examples of such apparent collusion with doctors and health care organizations come to mind, which may be illegal under federal statute and, if not illegal, are certainly a betrayal of the trust patients put in their physicians. Both these examples concern whistleblowers who stepped forward similar to the Oregon pharmaceutical rep who came to us.

One such whistleblower, who provided information to the US Department of Justice, accused the Bayer Corporation of inflating its wholesale costs for certain drugs in order to establish them as the basis for Medicaid reimbursements. Bayer then allegedly offered discounts off the wholesale prices to physicians, which meant doctors would be reimbursed at the phony higher rate and pocket the difference. The more prescriptions written, the higher the reimbursement, and the larger the Bayer market share.

In another example, John Foster, a national account manager for the Parke-Davis division of Warner-Lambert, was fired in 1999 after, he claimed, he had complained about $679,000 in cash and other incentives going to Ochsner Health Plan, a Louisiana-based health maintenance organization. In 2002, Pfizer, Inc., which had purchased Warner-Lambert, settled the case brought by the Justice Department for $49 million with whistleblower Foster receiving more than $3 million. In January 2002, the drug industry's trade association swore off these practices but only in the form of a "voluntary" code of ethics.

Illicit payments are one reason that the costs of prescription drugs have steadily increased at an average of 18 percent per annum. The introduction of new, blockbuster "miracle" drugs, as Prozac was dubbed, involves costly marketing campaigns that push that figure much higher. The great irony is that, unbeknown to the general public, most new drugs are not new at all but are reconfigurations of existing chemical compounds that are neither innovative nor lifesaving.

GlaxoSmithKline, for instance, changed the chemical structure of its antidepressant Wellbutrin, creating a "new" product, Wellbutrin XL, which was alleged to have new benefits but in actuality was the same drug. The company then noticed that its drug helped smokers quit, so it gained FDA approval to market it as Zyban—same drug, different approved use, more profit. Further, while the pharmaceutical companies go to great lengths to inform the public of the amount of money they spend developing these new drugs—portraying themselves as valiantly waging the war on illness and disease—they do not divulge *how* that money is spent. From my calculations, it's evident that approximately one-third to one-half of a drug company's budget is spent on advertising and that, in many cases, a large portion of a new drug's actual development cost—money they claim to be investing in the development of the drug—is underwritten by the NIH and other government programs and institutions. They will not reveal that taxpayers are often footing the bill to help develop these drugs, which sadly often aren't any safer or more effective and are being sold back to taxpayers at inflated prices.

Trying to get patients to switch brands is a more serious issue than just market-place competition. What we learned in our research into Prozac was that some patients have adverse reactions to it as an antidepressant. Similarly, the antidepressant S. K. was taking could be harmful to someone who is helped by Prozac. The side effects can be minor, but they can also be serious. What neither patients nor doctors need is the kind of bait-and-switch tactics employed by Lilly for Prozac, or as we are now seeing, direct-to-consumer drug advertising. Among the problems here is that the information about potential negative side effects in the advertising is less pronounced than it is on the drug packaging, which carries a black box warning.

Everyone has seen the ads: a tranquil stroll in the forest with singing birds, soft music, and an affectionate companion. The health risks in many ads are often downplayed, and the benefits are touted in such a way as to prompt patients to ask their doctors "if this drug is right" for them.

In addition to the problem of misleading advertising, there's also the literature that accompanies the product and information posted online. As we saw with Prozac and would see with many other drugs, the manufacturers routinely report and publish under the guise of medical literature the positive findings of drug studies, dismissing the disappointing ones and using language that has no practical informational value. The result is that patients in ever-increasing numbers are demanding and receiving prescriptions for medications they don't need and shouldn't be taking.

In all fairness, the ads do mention or refer to possible side effects for certain kinds of patients. But this is accomplished in quick-paced words in the TV spots and in minuscule type in the print versions. These ads, which must be successful or the companies wouldn't continue to spend billions on them, are problematic in other ways too. Under the influence of advertising, patients have been known to go "doctor shopping" until they find a physician who will write the prescriptions that they are looking for. According to the General Accounting Office (GAO) of Congress, an average of nearly ten million patients today have both requested and received a prescription for a drug after seeing an advertisement for it.

The FDA has promulgated regulations to prevent false or misleading advertising, but it does not have the legal authority to preapprove either the television commercials or the print ads and, in most cases, investigates only when a complaint is made, usually by a competitor.

The FDA's investigative staff was quite limited when we were litigating the Prozac Weekly case in 2002. Thus, the likelihood of an advertisement being deceptive was enormous. As of the writing of this book, the FDA appeals to health care professionals and consumers to report ads that appear deceptive through its "Bad Ad" and other reporting programs.

Although companies almost invariably remove or revise the misleading ad when confronted, I've seen occasions when they replace it with one that is more misleading. By the time the FDA gets around to the first complaint, the ad may have already completed its run and done its mischief, and the same is true if questions are raised about the replacement ad. It can typically take up to seventy-eight days from the time of the FDA complaint until a letter is sent to the offending company that lists the ways the commercial has to be changed to come into compliance. About a third of all TV pharmaceutical commercials run for two months or less.

Even so, some companies and some products are repeat offenders. Over the past decade, GlaxoSmithKline has received as many as fourteen letters from the FDA requiring changes in its advertising, Schering Corporation has received at least six, and Merck five. In one year alone, the FDA issued four letters to Glaxo, then Glaxo Wellcome, concerning its allergy nasal spray Flonase because of unsubstantiated claims and failure to provide information about major side effects. Similarly, the FDA sent four letters to Pfizer regarding its broadcast and print advertising for Lipitor.

As we would find with ads for Prozac Weekly, the characters and settings in many of the pharmaceutical ads deliberately convey benefits that a drug does not claim on its packaging. In at least one instance, it was discovered by the GAO that the television commercial's camera jumped about to distract the viewer from the announcer's words when he or she got to the information about who shouldn't take the drug and its negative side effects. It's wise to remember that, despite the horror stories I've been conveying about dangerous pharmaceuticals, most of them, when taken as prescribed, do what they claim to do. Though doctors are themselves the frequent victims of misinformation, they are the ones to whom a patient should listen to, not the voice of an actor in a television commercial. Did you know only two countries in the world permit direct-to-consumer drug advertising? Here and New Zealand. That's it.

In some instances, doctors can be their own worst enemies by their acceptance of what I consider thinly veiled pharmaceutical company bribery. Until recently, the freebies and gifts just kept coming: drug sales reps routinely gave incentives to physicians, nurses, and health care providers in the form of sample products, meals at expensive restaurants, tickets to concerts and sporting events, and "educational" seminars in vacation destinations. Litigation and new laws limiting the practices placed a spotlight on the disturbing practice: the more prescriptions written, the more benefits physicians received.

But I have found it goes far beyond just this. As I discovered while litigating a vaccine falsely purporting to prevent Lyme disease, many high-profile trend-setting physicians are covertly on a corporation's payroll or stand to profit handsomely by the successful launch of a new medical product. They accept honorariums, consultancy fees, and research grants in return for favorable endorsements and reviews of pharmaceutical products. Corporate scientists prepare the speeches that seemingly unbiased physicians delivered at medical conferences and ghostwrite the papers they publish in major medical journals. The new Physician Payment Sunshine Act that took effect in 2013 requires greater transparency and reporting, much to the chagrin of drug companies who protest it will cost too much to assemble the reports.

If such financial incentives did not pump up sales or compromise a physician's professional judgment, pharmaceutical companies wouldn't have been paying doctors off. But the truth is that the practice was, until recently, proven to be highly successful for drug manufacturers while the cost for it was passed on to consumers through the sale of overpriced drugs. As many physicians and experts in the field have told me, if the medical profession had stood up to pharmaceutical companies, older or generic drugs would be found to be as effective or more effective than the expensive new ones being marketed. As one example, a Harvard study showed that the popular diuretic Warfarin, sold as Coumadin, to combat conditions including blood clots which had been on the market for over ten years and costing less than 10¢ each, were at least as effective as and safer than newer, heavily advertised drugs including Pradaxa and Xarelto that sold for more and may have come with much greater risk.

As we got further into our Prozac Weekly case, we found evidence of this sort of cover-up and much more. We also obtained proof that the database provided to Lilly by doctors to market its new version of Prozac contained errors. This was the case for both sixteen-year-old G. M. and fifty-nine-year-old A. P. They were not taking any antidepressant medication—never had—had never been diagnosed as depressed, and had never had symptoms of depression. This was particularly frightening, as it shows we are at risk for having not only correct but also incorrect information about our health problems sold to the highest bidder.

The potential for privacy violation doesn't just end there. Employees at pharmacies and pharmaceutical companies, including data-processing clerks and anyone who happens to pick up the readouts, were able to access our clients' prescription histories or, as with A. P. and G. M., create fiction by cobbling together medical records from a variety of sources. Moreover, based on S. K.'s experience, samples were sent out from Walgreens by regular mail, not registered or certified, which meant that if the intended recipient had moved, the person now living at the address would get not only the drugs, but also private information about the former tenant or owner. Even more worrisome, if patients gave a business address, the samples would go there, increasing the likelihood that their medical conditions would be revealed to bosses and fellow employees.

Our suit asked for monetary damages to be paid to the members of the class, attorney fees to be paid for by the defendants, and, among other demands, for the defendants to be permanently barred from engaging in the alleged scheme. We also demanded that procedures be instituted that assure confidential prescription information be limited to purposes specifically authorized by members of the class. As we put it in our complaint: "Defendants' conduct was so outrageous in character and so extreme in degree as to go beyond all possible bounds of decency and can be regarded only as atrocious and utterly intolerable by a civilized society."

While we were waiting for our case to be heard—justice was moving especially slowly in our suit—troubling news of Eli Lilly's influence was forthcoming from Washington, DC. Big Pharma's robber barons were apparently in action again, only these robber barons were on steroids.

The event was the signing of the Homeland Security Act, which President Bush hailed as an "historic action" that demonstrated "the resolve of this great nation to defend our freedom, our security, and our way of life."[xx] No explanation was given for why, buried in this massive bill, was a provision that would protect Eli Lilly from lawsuits by parents whose children had been harmed by impurities found in its vaccines. Could the inclusion of this "get out of jail free" clause in the bill have been a result of Bush having appointed Lilly's CEO, Sidney Taurel, to a seat on his Homeland Security Advisory Council? What surprises were headed our way when we finally got to court with Prozac Weekly?

As Gary Farmer likes to say, sometimes our government moves like a race car and sometimes like a cruise ship. Where

Lilly litigation was concerned, the courts moved at a snail's pace. And with every passing day, sales of Prozac accumulated. Nearly three years elapsed before Judge Robert Andrews of Broward County, on May 16, 2005, dismissed our lawsuit in a fourteen-page decision granting summary judgment to the defendants and writing that he could find "no disclosure of plaintiffs' confidential and private medical information to anyone other than those authorized to receive that information."

Think about this for a minute. Communications between a patient and his or her physician and a patient's personal medical records are supposed to be kept confidential.

But the court declared that drug salespeople were perfectly within their rights to obtain such information and act on it as they saw fit, without permission from patients. Not only was this the incredible judgment of the courts—a classic case of a corporation's rights trumping an individual's—but in subsequent years, this practice has been further sanctioned by our courts. It has even become automated! The information can go directly to the Big Pharma reps via an Internet download.

In this way and without permission from physicians, drug manufacturers can find out which physicians are prescribing what drugs and whether patients are filling those prescriptions or not. They know details of people's medical conditions and lab tests, and sometimes their ages, income, and ethnic backgrounds—all on the alleged grounds that drug reps and the manufacturers they represent can be sure that the "right" drugs are given to the "right" patients.[xxi, xxii] Conversely, legitimate scientific researchers and physicians cannot consult pharmaceutical company records or review clinical trial data to find out if the "right" drug is really the wrong drug. In whose interest have these measures been put into place?

To this very day, we do not know whether Holy Cross Hospital or the four signatories to the letter or both were paid by Lilly. S. K. says Dr. Lambert told her that the medical group provided signed letterhead for Lilly and let Lilly write the contents, a practice that was pioneered by debt-collection agencies, where bill collectors sometimes pay public officials to use their letterhead. It's a betrayal by the institutions we place our trust in. Whether or not the medical group members or anyone at the hospital had ultimate approval of the content, we don't know. We also cannot think of any explanation that would be exculpatory. Neither do we know how many people got the "congratulations" letter—whether it was in the hundreds or the thousands—or how many would have received it if S. K. hadn't gone to a lawyer.

We lost this case, but we were far from letting Lilly get away with what we believed to be flagrant disregard for patients' rights. We came back at them again, only this time we were armed with documents that proved what we had previously only suspected.

CHAPTER 3

The "Cure" May Be the Problem

S. K. IN BROWARD COUNTY was not the only one who got the
Walgreen's mailing for Prozac, but she got angry and called an
attorney about it. Others followed S. K.'s lead. Among them was
a group of Lilly sales representatives, some of whom were pharmacists, who saw me interviewed on television about our Prozac
case. They were troubled by what I had to say and felt compelled
to expose pharmaceutical industry fraud that was beyond even
what I had imagined possible. Gary Farmer and I, joined by attorney Michael Freedland from Gary's office, would ultimately
work with the whistleblowers for nearly a decade. The first of
several new cases that came as a result was Lilly's illegal marketing of the drug Zyprexa, an antipsychotic that accounted for a
nearly a third of the company's revenue in 2003, with worldwide
sales totaling near $40 billion.

What's important to understand about Zyprexa is its incredible financial performance though it has dubious success as a safe
and effective medical treatment. This isn't the paradox it first

appears to be. Former *New England Journal of Medicine* (NEJM) editor Marcia Angell described the process succinctly:

> Suppose you are a big pharmaceutical company. You make a drug that is approved for a very limited use…How could you turn it into a blockbuster…You could simply market the drug for unapproved ("off-label") uses—despite the fact that doing so is illegal. You do that by carrying out "research" that falls way below the standard required for FDA approval, then "educating" doctors about any favorable results. That way, you could circumvent the law. You could say you were not marketing for unapproved uses; you were merely disseminating the results of research to doctors—who can legally prescribe a drug for any use. But it would be bogus education about bogus research. It would really be marketing.[xxiii]

This, we would discover, was exactly what Lilly had done with Zyprexa and had likely done earlier with Prozac. One of the many problems with this type of fraud is that prescription drugs can cause more problems than the condition or disease that they're designed to treat. Moreover, the negative side effects of one prescription can send patients to consult their doctors about the "new" condition, only to be prescribed yet another drug that can produce still more negative side effects.

At the risk of sounding alarmist, let me share a statistic: the negative side effects from drugs send approximately 4.5 million Americans to the doctor's office or the emergency room each year—far more than for common conditions such as infection, strep throat, or pneumonia.[xxiv] These reactions are, according to the National Academy of Sciences, Engineering, and Medicine's Institute of Medicine, the fourth leading cause of hospital deaths, topped only by heart disease, cancer, and stroke.[xxv]

If that doesn't frighten you, maybe this will: researchers at the Indiana University School of Medicine used a computer program to analyze 5,600 drug labels and more than five hundred thousand labeled effects. The study found, on average, a "mind-numbing" seventy potential negative drug reactions for each drug studied. The most commonly prescribed drugs averaged around one hundred side effects each, with some drugs containing as many as 525 listed reactions.[xxvi] As should come as no surprise, medications typically used by psychiatrists and neurologists have the most complex potential drug reactions and side effects. Some are garden variety, like vomiting, anxiety, arrhythmia, irregular or fast heartbeat, difficulty swallowing or breathing, seizures, fever, or persistent sweating. Some can be disabling and permanent: diabetes, dystonia (movement disorder), neuroleptic syndrome (neurologic disorder), shaky leg syndrome, tardive dyskinesia (frightening involuntary body movements and tics), hypogonadism (low testosterone), and, as we've mentioned, suicidal ideation and "a desire to kill."

Negative side effects aside, it gets worse. The "success" of one drug, spawns other drugs. Because of Prozac's and then Zyprexa's meteoric success, along came other atypical or second-generation antipsychotics, with each competing company developing a version of their own: Geodon (Parke-Davis/

Pfizer), Seroquel (AstraZeneca), Abilify (Bristol-Myers Squibb), Invega and Risperdal (Johnson and Johnson /Janssen), and others. Although far more expensive than Thorazine, Haldol, and Perphenazine, and the first generation of antipsychotics they replaced, their attraction was based on the widely held perception in the medical community that they were safer to use and could thus be prescribed more widely. At least this is what the marketing departments of drug companies declared.

Whether these drugs are actually safer or more effective is a much-debated point, and I'll not argue the pros and cons except to say that both generations of drugs are said to work in essentially the same way: by blocking dopamine and serotonin receptors in the brain to reduce manic and delusional behavior. They do not cure the underlying conditions they are prescribed for but effectively mask the symptoms. This can be beneficial when an out-of-control patient must be chemically restrained, but problematic in the long term, as patients and physicians can be lulled into believing that the underlying condition has improved when this isn't the case. The important difference is that psychiatric wards were the primary domain of Thorazine and Haldol, while prescriptions for Zyprexa and its near cousins are filled most commonly at your local pharmacy.

From a marketing point of view, the timing was right for an atypical antipsychotic feeding frenzy. Patents for Big Pharma's star hitters, SSRIs and antidepressants, were near running out. What would fill the void? The rise of these new psychotropic drugs was a potential gold mine. Predictably, an intense competition among manufacturers ensued, putting pressure on sales reps whose managers demanded or at least tacitly approved of them bending the rules. They were aware that doctors were allowed to prescribe drugs off-label (meaning, as I've said, for uses not approved by the FDA) but it was, and is, a criminal violation to market these drugs to physicians for off-label uses. It is one thing to prescribe a drug off-label when it is completely necessary—when there are no alternatives and someone could suffer grave injury to his or her health. But that was not the case for most of the prescriptions being written for Zyprexa and most of the antipsychotics. Big Pharma management's attitude was that if you couldn't or wouldn't aggressively push doctors to prescribe these drugs off-label, you needed to look for another line of work.

Based almost exclusively on questionable Eli Lilly–funded testing, the FDA approved Zyprexa in 1996 for the short-term treatment of schizophrenia, and in 2000 for the long-term treatment of schizophrenia and bipolar and manic disorders. Zyprexa quickly became the industry's best-selling antipsychotic and Lilly's first billion-dollar drug. As is the case with so many other pharmaceuticals approved for one condition and used for another, Zyprexa was heavily prescribed off-label, most notably for depression, anxiety, and panic attacks. This practice was so popular that psychiatrists eventually began recommending it for children and teens whom they determined were crying too often, suffered from insomnia, or had trouble concentrating at work or in school. Unbelievable but still true, a cousin of this drug would eventually be recommended for "compulsive shopping disorder."[xxvii]

Did we learn nothing from off-label marketing in the past? I am reminded, in this regard, of my litigation over DES, a synthetic estrogen, which was promoted off-label in the 1950s, 1960s and into the beginning of 1970 to hundreds of thousands of women with menstrual problems, morning sickness, infertility, and even something described as "excess height disorder." So popular was DES that some companies were even adding it to vitamin tablets! The tragedy is that it didn't help a single one of the prescribed or off-label conditions, and its side effects included cancer and reproductive abnormalities that were passed from one generation to the next.

Zyprexa's off-label uses were also questioned. Powerful as the drug was as a mood stabilizer, patients began reporting a wide range of negative side effects, most notably excessive sleep, rapid weight gain, diabetes and diabetic precursor conditions such as hyperglycemia (high blood sugar), pancreatitis in which the pancreas shuts down, sexual dysfunction, and tardive dyskinesia, a disorder resulting in involuntary, repetitive Parkinson's-like symptoms such as nervous twitches and uncontrollable tics. The truly insidious thing about such negative side effects is that even if you stop taking the drugs, there are many instances when the condition it has caused cannot be cured, and the longer you take the drug, the more likely you are to develop the problems.

If I haven't frightened you yet, this may: when used long term, Zyprexa and other so-called second-generation atypical antipsychotics may induce or increase the likelihood of psychotic behavior and suicide because it's thought to shrink the frontal lobe of the brain. As Dr. Nancy Anderson, the former editor-in-chief of the *American Journal of Psychiatry*, reported, the more of these drugs a patient ingests, the more brain tissue is lost and the greater the cognitive impairment. By solving one problem for a period of time, others were likely to appear.[xviii] The truth of the matter is that many psychotropic drugs create a rebound effect that mimics the condition that was the basis for the original prescription, thereby creating an endless loop of symptoms, creating the perpetual patient or client.[xxix] Children prescribed an antipsychotic to help control their behavior might, over time, find themselves with chronic mental illnesses.

The bad news about Zyprexa became public in 2001, despite heavy lobbying by Lilly. In November, the *Journal of the American Medical Association*, the FDA's Center for Drug Evaluation and Research, and a prominent Duke University Medical Center physician linked Zyprexa with hyperglycemia in adolescents. FDA committee members subsequently published a report in December in *The American Journal of Medicine* linking Zyprexa to diabetes. The following year, British and Japanese researchers reported similar side effects, and finally, in 2003, the FDA demanded that Zyprexa carry a black-box warning, the strongest warning label possible for prescription drugs. With the new warning came new litigation. As a result of the publicity about the new black-box warning, individuals who developed diabetes started filing lawsuits all over the United States. Those lawsuits began in 2003 and 2004.

Having already taken a major pharmaceutical company to court, I was hesitant to join what could have become a stampede of Zyprexa cases. There were too many challenges, not the least of which was the fact that Lilly was one of largest and most influential drug companies in the world and, as we had seen with the Homeland Security Act, had paid confederates at all levels of the government and its regulatory agencies.

What promised to be an equally great obstacle was the large body of research and testing that Eli Lilly paid to have done on Zyprexa and the articles it had sponsored or ghostwritten; those materials had achieved the level of medical consensus and was used by the courts to determine what the jury could hear and what it could not. In other words, I wouldn't be able to introduce evidence and testimony if it contradicted what Lilly declared the facts to be. Difficult as this may be to believe, and contradictory to what you see on television courtroom dramas, it's the reality and warrants explanation.

The 1923 *Frye v. United States* ruling permits the introduction of scientific evidence only if it has "general acceptance" in the relevant scientific community. The *Daubert v. Merrell Dow* ruling, which came seventy years later, permits scientific evidence to be introduced in court if it meets the judge's standards for reliability. Thus, if a pharmaceutical company can publish enough peer-reviewed journal articles claiming its products are safe, expert testimony cannot be presented to the contrary. Never mind that the pharmaceutical companies themselves invariably write these articles, pay physician shills to put their names on them, and use financial inducements to encourage journal editors to publish them.

To describe the matter as simply as possible, if the Frye rule had been around in Galileo's time, his assertion that the world was round would not have been admitted in court because it was contrary to the scientific consensus of his day. Under Daubert, Galileo might get his day in court, but only if the judge decided his scientific studies followed the then-accepted research methods that had already proven the earth was flat.

Herein lies a major challenge in going after corporations as big as Lilly in today's legal climate A corporate defendant can spend hundreds of millions of dollars to pay for clinical trials, research studies, and journal articles that influence what a judge will use to determine what constitutes the medical consensus. Plaintiffs, on the other hand, don't have the funds to conduct their own drug trials or underwrite research that may be favorable to their cases. They are also greatly limited by what expert witnesses they can call upon to testify on their behalves. Unless their expert witnesses have adhered to the methodology and practices of their consensus peers, they will be barred from addressing juries. They cannot challenge the status quo unless they are members of the status quo to a degree.

Yet another challenge we faced with Zyprexa litigation was the labeling on the pill bottles, which listed the negative side effects alleged by plaintiffs. The defendants could and would argue that they had never made a secret of what could happen when taking the drug. This is precisely why ever-increasing lists of negative side effects in ever-smaller print are included with prescription purchases. The purpose is not only to warn the user of the negative side effects, but to also try and build a legal fire-wall to keep from being sued.

Finally, there was the added difficulty of proving that the most pronounced Zyprexa side effect, diabetes, was an actual result of taking the drug. Research as far back as the 1920s noted a connection between schizophrenia and diabetes, and more recent testing showed that schizophrenics developed diabetes at a rate four times higher than that of the general population, regardless of whether they used antipsychotic drugs. Proving the connection to Zyprexa could be a time-consuming and very expensive proposition.

Gary Farmer and I were weighing the pros and cons of taking Lilly back to court and how we might overcome these obstacles when we spoke at length with sales rep James Wetta and other current and former Lilly drug sales reps who had helped us with our Prozac Weekly case. They hadn't shed much new light on how Lilly marketed Prozac, but what they had to say about the Zyprexa marketing scheme came as a revelation.

CHAPTER 4

What the Whistleblowers
Have to Say

STUDIES HAVE REVEALED THAT OVER half of all Americans have witnessed or been pressured to commit wrongdoing at their workplaces.ˣˣˣ They are nurses who have observed medical malpractice, salesmen who have been advised to lie about product safety or reliability, accountants who have discovered financial fraud, teachers who have been pressured to inflate student test scores, and lab technicians who have been told to suppress negative test results. Examples are too numerous to tally. Yet the number of people willing to step forward to expose these betrayals are remarkably few. The most conservative estimates place that number at less than 2 percent. Less than 1 percent actually put their livelihoods on the line to come forward. James Wetta and several of his current and former Lilly colleagues are among them.

Wetta, a thirty-six-year-old husband and father, had worked as a drug rep for other pharmaceutical companies before joining

Eli Lilly in 2000, where he specialized in Central Nervous System (CNS) drugs. During his tenure, there was an important change in how these drugs were being marketed. Though Zyprexa had once been promoted to psychiatrists by a dedicated CNS specialty–sales force, it was being widely marketed to primary care practitioners for issues that weren't approved by the FDA or listed in the Zyprexa package insert. The sales team Wetta joined, for example, was dedicated to selling the drug off-label to the non-schizophrenic elderly for symptoms commonly associated with Alzheimer's disease and dementia. Profits were the motivation, not patient safety.

Most important for our case, Wetta maintained that Lilly had failed to give patients and physicians adequate warning of Zyprexa's negative side effects. It did this by submitting misleading information to the FDA and distorting and burying disclaimers in fine print. Lilly had also boosted drug sales by arranging with physicians and caregivers to switch patients' medications without their approval or knowledge. And this was just the beginning of even more egregious conduct.

Lilly sales reps, Wetta said, targeted mental patients who were too medicated to reasonably know what drugs were being given to them. He said that Lilly had also purposefully designed its marketing campaign to include children too young to be diagnosed as suffering from acute mania. Children in the foster care system were also mentioned specifically, as this subgroup didn't necessarily have guardians who were in a position to supervise what medications were being given to their children. When Wetta complained to Lilly's marketing director about these sales tactics in 2002, he was told to either join the program or look for another job.

We learned from the whistleblowers that such treatment is typical of the pharmaceutical industry. Rather than dialogue with an employee or provide workers a forum where concerns can be safely expressed, employers routinely stifle criticism. The employee becomes marginalized and suspect in the eyes of coworkers until he or she chooses to quit. This was the case with Wetta. After two years of complaining about shady sales tactics, he packed his things and took a job selling real estate.

Fellow salesman Robert Rudolph also left Lilly, only he had been with the company for decades. One of the things that offended him the most was how sales reps were allowed into doctors' offices on weekends to collect names of patients taking certain drugs in hopes of switching them to Lilly products. "I was put in a position of breaking the law, in my view, or quitting," he told us.

Rudolph approached another Lilly sales rep, Hector Rosado, who in turn contacted others. They didn't just have stories to tell; they also had documents to back up their claims. Among the most damning were reports of drug trials that linked Zyprexa to suicide. In five premarketing clinical trials conducted by Lilly involving 2,500 patients, twelve patients committed suicide, making Zyprexa the drug with the highest suicide rate of any antipsychotic in clinical history. As one of our expert witnesses would later testify, Lilly suppressed data on suicidal acts from these trials and thus increased the likelihood that the drug would be prescribed to at-risk children.

Sadly, many of the documents that I have personally examined—documents showing how Lilly manipulated test results and spun the data—cannot be made public to this day, as they are deemed confidential and are still under court seal. The penalty for breaching confidentiality can mean jail time or a heavy fine. This was the experience of clinical drug trial reviewer Dr. David Egilman, a professor at Brown University's Department of Community Health. Driven by a desire to reveal important health information contained in the Zyprexa documents, he leaked several on the Internet and was fined $100,000. This was payable, of course, to Eli Lilly.[xxxi]

In court, however, we could and ultimately did use the documents. Equally important to our case were the personal stories of Wetta and the others. Most shocking was Wetta's claim that he and another drug salesman had been on a specialized, long-term care Lilly task force whose sole purpose was to distribute rebate checks and other perks while extolling the drug's effectiveness for a litany of nonindicated uses, most specifically to sedate, elderly nursing home residents exhibiting symptoms of agitation, anxiety, and insomnia.

Literature and sales tools were tailored specifically for this purpose, as was a colorful visual ad showing drowsy and sleeping seniors enjoying their golden years in the tranquility of a well-appointed nursing home. To accompany the glossy brochures, sales reps were provided with preapproved responses to what the company knew in advance would be difficult selling points. If a psychiatrist asked about the negative side effects of Zyprexa, she was instructed to say that the drug was primarily a mood stabilizer that, if taken in combination with antidepressants to mitigate negative side effects, would bring positive results.

In this way, Lilly reps promoted the use of Lilly's drug in combination with other pharmaceuticals, what the industry refers to as "polypharmacy" or "drug cocktails"—the condition that one drug created could simply and effectively be solved by adding another to the mix. Such a drug cocktail was, as you may remember, what had been prescribed to seven-year-old Gabriel Myers when he took his own life in his foster family's bathroom. One of the bonuses, from the drug manufacturer's perspective, is that by mixing the pharmaceuticals, it makes it more difficult for a judge and jury to determine which of the drugs caused injury or death.

Using these and other sales tools, a dangerous and powerful antipsychotic was promoted to people for whom the drug had no other health benefit than to put them to as a sleep aid but had the potential side effects of diminishing mental capacity and increasing risk of diabetes, heart attack, and seizure. The overall message to sales reps was "Push the drug and change the prescription, and bonuses are yours." Patients were not informed of the financial incentives of their physicians or care providers for changing or adding to their prescriptions, and some patients were never told that they were actually being given the drug.

Those brochure ads of seniors enjoying the tranquility of their golden years couldn't have been further from the truth considering how this drug and so many other antipsychotics were often being used: as a chemical restraint, a convenient tool for nursing home staff or others entrusted with eldercare. "Five at five" was the Zyprexa sales pitch: five milligrams dispensed at 5:00 p.m. would keep a patient quiet all evening.

At $10 a pill, the return for Lilly was astronomical. Zyprexa brought in an estimated $400 million in new revenue and a 40 percent gain in new sales attributed directly to off-label usage. It was impossible for Gary and I to calculate the human toll in the number of damaged lives, even without factoring in those patients who legitimately needed to be treated with the drug and became diabetic or suffered from diabetic-related complications or pancreatitis. Even more insidious, as the whistleblowers told us, was that while Lilly had been misrepresenting Zyprexa's risk of causing weight gain, suspecting it contributed to diabetes, the company had enjoyed prominent sales of its insulin drugs. In other words, Zyprexa-related weight gain ostensibly boosted other Lilly drug sales.

To what lengths would the company go to protect its market share? The answer to that question was evident in the experience of Kentucky Medicaid prescribers in 2002. Because Zyprexa cost approximately twice that of similar drugs and showed little evidence of being superior to its competitors, state prescribers decided to exclude it from their preferred list of drugs. To their shock and embarrassment, the nonprofit National Alliance for the Mentally Ill (NAMI) spoke out against the decision, placed full-page ads in newspapers, barraged state officials with letters, called for hearings, and bused protesters to those hearings.[xxxii] Unprepared for such a show of force, officials quickly reinstated Zyprexa on the preferred pharmaceuticals list. What was not revealed until the following year was that the entire NAMI campaign—including newspaper ads, a letter-writing campaign, and busloads of protesters—was paid for by Lilly. NAMI was funded to the tune of $11.7 million by drug companies, and Lilly was the largest donor. The drug company's largesse included loaning NAMI a Lilly executive who worked at NAMI headquarters and whose salary was paid for by the company.[xxxiii]

As investigative journalist Ken Silverstein would write, deceit was the name of the game. Here was a trendsetting and influential mental health nonprofit whose grass roots were being watered by Lilly's millions.

CHAPTER 5

Indicting Big Pharma

BASED ON WHAT WETTA AND the others shared with Gary and me, I decided to forgo what had become the accepted model in pharmaceutical litigation: gather as many clients as one could and then prove the drug had unreasonably harmed them. Rather, I wanted to show how one pharmaceutical company had wantonly committed fraud on hundreds of thousands, perhaps millions, of its customers. It had actively and purposefully engaged in a nationwide campaign to sell Zyprexa to a class of people for whom its drug was unapproved. The company had minimized and misrepresented the drug's dangers and placed profits above public safety. Further, if we convinced judge and jury of how one company conducted business, perhaps the entire industry would come under scrutiny.

With exposure as our goal, we decided to try a litigation strategy driven by lessons I had learned taking on the tobacco industry a decade earlier. Previous attempts to beat the tobacco giants in court had failed primarily because plaintiffs could not prove that smoking alone caused cancer, and even if it did, "buyer beware" warning labels made it a moot point. The ill or injured knew what risks they were taking—or such was the claim.

I adopted a radically different approach when I filed my tobacco company litigation. After several false starts and in conjunction with other attorneys bringing suit, I went after the tobacco companies on the grounds of fraud. My aim was to prove that so-called low-tar, light cigarettes were even more dangerous than regular cigarettes and the cigarette companies knew it. We also chose not to take the cigarette manufacturers on single-handedly but to partner with the US government or, more precisely, forty-six of the fifty states as co-plaintiffs.

Partnering with the government had made perfect sense. This is because taxpayers pick up so much of the financial burden related to medical conditions brought on by smoking through such programs as Medicaid and Medicare. From a political view, the idea was also a highly attractive one, for by the time I got to court in the mid-1990s, the majority of the public mistrusted cigarette companies. Best of all, from the state's side, the costs of pursuing the litigation were completely underwritten by private counsel—myself and other law firms. Should the private counsel recoup money, the state would keep all returns less our legal fees. This was not exactly an incentive for most attorneys at the time, but it was enough for me. I was passionate about stopping the cigarette companies from selling their poison, and for the first time ever, the tobacco companies were held financially accountable for their lies. The strategy I put in place was then carried on by others and is now being employed overseas to try and rein in the industry.

For our tobacco litigation, we filed class action charges under state consumer fraud statutes. This time around, with our pharmaceutical industry litigation, we utilized a rarely used federal law that dated back to the Civil War. The Federal False Claims Act, also known as the Lincoln Law, was written to impose liability on persons and companies, typically federal contractors, who defrauded government programs by charging outrageous prices or selling inferior products, from horses and blankets to hammers. Similarly, Eli Lilly had harmed the American taxpayer by defrauding Medicare and Medicaid by selling products it knew to be inferior. The concept was a good one, though this would be the first time it would be used to take on a major pharmaceutical company.

Among the False Claims Act's other provisions is a whistleblower clause known as *qui tam*, which is a Latin phrase going back to medieval times meaning "he who sues on behalf of the king." Today, this whistleblower clause allows people who are not working for the government to file actions on behalf of or in partnership with the government. By partnering with the government and filing in this manner, we could not only steer the litigation ourselves, but we could also provide our chief witnesses—James Wetta and our other whistleblowers—with government protections and financial incentives. If we were successful, Wetta and the others could collect a share of whatever settlement or penalty might be imposed on Lilly.

The downside of the plan was that our firm would have to shoulder the expense of preparing and taking the case to court and, if we lost, might be out several hundred thousand or perhaps even a million dollars. It was quite a risk to take considering that the lion's share of any settlement would naturally go to the American taxpayer, on whose behalf we were bringing suit. Moreover, it was quite a risk for Wetta and the fellow whistleblowers. The moment the court made our case public, they would become pariahs in the corporate world, let alone among their pharmaceutical salesmen friends and colleagues. Nevertheless, we moved ahead with our suit.

My plan from the start was to file in federal court in Philadelphia because the US attorney's office here had particular expertise in health care fraud. Paradoxically, I wouldn't be going to my own state's attorney because Pennsylvania is not one of the 29 states that has passed a False Claims statue. To find out why our taxpayers (and consumers of prescription drugs in 21 states) would not be eligible to receive such compensation, you would have to ask our Big Pharma-friendly legislature.

Thankfully, the doors at our US attorney's office were open to us. US Attorney for the Eastern District of Pennsylvania and future congressman Pat Meehan, Assistant US Attorney for the Eastern District of Pennsylvania Laurie Magid, and assistant US attorney Joseph Trautwein welcomed us into their offices, interviewed Wetta, and examined our documents. They were also outraged by Lilly's behavior and agreed to partner with us.

As our case developed, we teamed up with former assistant Philadelphia district attorney Mike Mustokoff of the Duane

Morris law firm. Several years later, U.S. Department of Justice attorneys would take responsibility for pursuing the case, joining with us. Among them were Assistant US Attorneys Virginia A. Gibson and Margaret Hutchinson. With their backing and support, we were also able to avail ourselves of help from the Departments of Justice and Health and the Human Resources (HHS) and the Health Care Fraud Prevention and Enforcement Action Team (HEAT). They provided trained personnel to help us investigate our claims and assigned Joseph Trautwein to the case.

As part of a False Claims Act prosecution, different departments of the government get involved in the investigation, sometimes including the FBI, health fraud and FDA investigators, the Office of the Inspector of the General (OIG), and others. Of equal importance is having a federal judge supervising the investigation. And as previously alluded to, under the judge's watch, the complaint is kept under seal as the case is being built. Eventually, a subpoena of materials is requested, which is usually the first time the defendant is put on notice that it is under investigation for civil and/or criminal conduct. Until the subpoena and the grand jury that may follow, the defendant has no knowledge of the content and scope of the investigation. The defendant doesn't know, for example, if there's a whistleblower involved, a False Claims Act allegation, or something else. The seal remains in place, sometimes for years, during the time the government and law firms gather the evidence leading to civil and criminal charges that can ultimately end in criminal indictment and/or civil settlements to resolve the case.

It was while our whistleblower False Claims Act claim was still under seal that I received an unexpected update from Wetta, who by this time had left the real estate business—the California market had collapsed—and had become a salesman for one of Lilly's competitors, pharmaceutical giant AstraZeneca, located in Wilmington, Delaware. As Wetta's identity as a whistleblower was still secret, he had had no trouble finding another job as a drug rep.

"Steve, I can't believe it," he told me. "It's going on here too."

Wetta's reference was to the marketing of AstraZeneca's drug Seroquel, another atypical antipsychotic that had become nearly as popular as Zyprexa.

CHAPTER 6

When One Antidepressant Alone Isn't Enough

AT THIS POINT IN MY Eli Lilly suit, I was already stretched thin. There were still many witnesses to depose, research to conduct, drug trials to study, and briefs to write. Moreover, the cost of underwriting our litigation with Lilly was costing my firm hundreds of thousands of dollars, with more spending to come. This was money that we would recoup if we won our case, but there was no guarantee that we would. Still, I took the time to hear Wetta out, and I was glad I did.

His story was frighteningly similar to what he had told us about the Lilly sales department. Seroquel, approved by the FDA in 2000 for the treatment of schizophrenia and in 2004 for the short-term treatment of acute manic episodes associated with bipolar disorder, was being heavily marketed for off-label use.

In an effort to reach children, brand managers had gone so far as to discuss creating *Winnie-the-Pooh*-inspired characters of Tigger (bipolar) and Eeyore (depressed) to sell Seroquel and like many other drug companies, produced an array of child-friendly marketing items emblazoned with product logos.[xxxiv]

Just as Lilly had done, AstraZeneca had put together specialized sales teams. One team's chief purpose was to market the drug to inmates, soldiers, and the elderly for unapproved uses. The drug was being used in the treatment of Alzheimer's disease, post-traumatic stress disorder, depression, sleeplessness, ADD, and even to help with anger management. When the team identified a psychiatrist who was willing to go the distance with them, the results were spectacular. In one year alone, the top ten Pennsylvania prescribers wrote nearly nineteen thousand prescriptions for Seroquel, costing Medicaid $3.6 million.

I wasn't going to turn a blind eye to these allegations. Nor was I going to pass off the heavy lifting to another firm. I already had the contacts with state and federal attorneys' offices to file another Federal False Claims Act case, a team of lawyers who were now steeped in the nuances of pharmaceutical litigation, and medical experts who were willing to testify about the dangers of antipsychotic drugs. The same people who were helping us with Zyprexa could help with Seroquel. Never mind that I might go bankrupt while trying to win the case.

With the Zyprexa suit under government seal (meaning Lilly had no idea of what was coming), we once again filed a case with James Wetta as a whistleblower in the matter of AstraZeneca and Seroquel. As in the Zyprexa case, we filed a Federal False Claims Act and charges under the Anti-Kickback Statute. This time, we charged that AstraZeneca had provided illegal remuneration to physicians and caregivers to promote Seroquel. Often $1,000 or more was paid as a bonus for writing more prescriptions for the drug and promoting others to do so as well; they were often given money as paid speakers as well, but the real money was paid for increased prescribing.

The marching orders for the doctors were to target colleagues who did not typically treat schizophrenia or bipolar disorder, such as eldercare, primary care, and pediatric physicians, and those supervising prison inmates and working in veterans' hospitals. The purpose of these consultations was to verbally encourage the unapproved use of Seroquel without the drug company having to make written claims it knew were not true. In other words, it hired a reputable spokesperson to do its dirty work.

We obtained documents through discovery showing that AstraZeneca had knowingly manipulated the ways test results were presented to the public. The company claimed, for instance, that patients taking Seroquel lost weight and were less prone to diabetes than those taking competing drugs such as Zyprexa, Geodon, and Risperdal, when in fact its own studies revealed the opposite: patients on Seroquel gained an average of eleven pounds a year and the drug was directly linked to diabetes. Positive studies were hyped while negative ones were filed away.

"The larger issue is how do we face the outside world when they begin to criticize us for suppressing data," wrote John Tumas, AstraZeneca's publications manager at the time, in an e-mail in 1999. "We must find a way to diminish the negative findings."

We could, in essence, convict AstraZeneca using its own words. We could also convincingly show how AstraZeneca's bad behavior had cost the American taxpayers hundreds of millions of dollars each year. Besides the Medicaid and Medicare reimbursements that were still being paid to AstraZeneca, the Pentagon was spending hundreds of millions each year dispensing Seroquel to soldiers fighting in Iraq and Afghanistan. According to the Department of Veterans Affairs, the Pentagon had already spent $850 million on Seroquel, with nearly 100 percent of the prescriptions written for off-label disorders. Moreover, these figures were in addition to what was paid to the Bureau of Prisons on behalf of inmates.

We would file yet another whistleblower/False Claims Act case, this time against pharmaceutical giant Pfizer for the illegal marketing of its drugs Geodon, Bextra, Zyvox, and Lyrica. Thus, in the process of building not one but three major pharmaceutical cases, our firm grew to include several dozen attorneys working on our behalf, many of them in temporary, rented offices. Had I not won major settlements against the tobacco companies and established partnerships with other counsel, our small firm may have gone under. And all of this, you may remember, had grown out of my pro bono association with Gary Farmer during the *Bush v. Gore* 2000 election litigation, which had led us to take on Lilly for its marketing of Prozac Weekly. As I will repeat once again, we don't have to see the larger picture to set the wheels in motion. Merely taking the first step, even if it's against a Goliath, will often trigger events well beyond our imaginations.

I will save the reader from a lengthy recital of the specifics of our new cases here because you've heard the major points already. Pfizer did much the same as Eli Lilly and AstraZeneca, hyping the positive studies of its drugs and burying the negative. Further, Pfizer's marketing teams, one of which was fittingly called "the Sharks," were dedicated to using the same off-label sales practices as those of its competitors. Their marching orders were to "grow share," a phrase used at training meetings meaning to expand beyond the FDA-approved guidelines. Profits were the motivation and patient safety not a consideration.

Pfizer also provided funding to physician spokesmen for the National Alliance for the Mentally Ill to promote Geodon, its atypical antipsychotic, to children. The spokesmen appeared on behalf of the nonprofit without telling their audiences of fellow physicians and concerned families that they were actually on the Pfizer payroll.

The only big difference between Pfizer and its competitors was that Pfizer had been down this road before with its illegal marketing of its painkiller Neurontin. As part of its 2004 settlement, Pfizer had signed a corporate integrity agreement promising never to use such sales tactics again. According to our whistleblowers, Pfizer's behavior hadn't changed except for perhaps becoming more adept at breaking the law and bending the rules. Pfizer illegally paid physicians recruitment bonuses of amounts varying from $250 to $1,000 a day to attend meetings to promote Pfizer drugs, $500 to help another physician "review" a clinical paper supporting a Pfizer position, and $250 to $1,500 a day for travel and meal expenses to attend conferences in luxury hotels, where they could meet and mingle with their colleagues. In one case, Pfizer paid a physician $4,000 a day to use his personal helicopter to go from one off-label marketing event to another.[xxxv] Perpetuating this fraud was deemed by the company to be "the cost of doing business." It seems the pain and injury this drug and others caused was a matter of business as usual too.

I felt a combination of pride, satisfaction, and anxiety when the Justice Department finally unsealed our complaints. To my knowledge, never before had one law firm, and a small one at that, made such an aggressive effort to hold so many multinational pharmaceutical corporations accountable. Nor had any other firm presented such a significant body of evidence to support its claims.

We might have submitted even more evidence had we not decided to move forward when we did. By this time, James Wetta had left AstraZeneca and was about to be hired by Merck, where salesmen may have been operating under the same marching orders. However, like a spy coming in from the cold, Wetta was greatly relieved to finally go public. Not only had he been operating undercover for over half a decade, but his home had also been under surveillance. He was worried for his wife and daughter. The drug companies knew or suspected by this time that an informant was at work; they just didn't know who or how far-reaching the investigation.

Our celebration of what came next was a private one, for the press was not informed of how we built our cases nor were they introduced to the attorneys who did the actual work. Instead, the

Justice Department held the press conferences and took all the credit. The only exception was a brief thank you to my office in our suit against Lilly from Assistant U.S. Attorney Charlene K. Fullmer, who would go on to partner with us in our next major case. She now supervises and prosecutes health care and fraud matters as Deputy Chief for Affirmative Litigation in the Civil Division of the United States Attorney's Office in the Eastern District of Pennsylvania.

In January of 2009, Lilly pleaded guilty to illegally marketing Zyprexa and, by previous agreement, settled civil suits for $1.42 billion, the largest amount ever paid by any one defendant at that time and the largest single drug settlement in US history. Six hundred million of this was a criminal penalty for pleading guilty to a misdemeanor. This remarkable record only stood for eight months, until Pfizer too decided to settle, this time to the tune of $2.3 billion. This figure included $1.3 billion in criminal penalties, which set a world record. Early the following year, our AstraZeneca/Seroquel case settled for $520 million. In all, we were instrumental in recovering over $4 billion in just a few years. But even these figures would pale in comparison to what was coming next—taking on America's undisputed pharmaceutical kingpin: Johnson & Johnson.

CHAPTER 7

Exposing the Betrayal

WHEN I BEGAN MY CAREER, I could never have imagined that a firm I headed would win three back-to-back record-breaking pharmaceutical *qui tam* whistleblower cases. I was justifiably proud of the accomplishment but still had to ask myself if our litigation had actually changed pharmaceutical companies' behavior.

The settlements we won temporarily lowered the market shares of three giant drug producers and put several billion dollars back into federal and state treasuries, yet none of the corporate officers who put their companies into jeopardy were held personally accountable. Executives were not asked to return the millions of dollars in bonuses and stock options they'd received, and none were charged with criminal behavior. And though these companies were forced to sign corporate integrity agreements, our experience with Pfizer—and again later with AstraZeneca— had taught us that such agreements weren't enforced. It was a Pyrrhic victory, a single battle won in the midst of a war we were losing.

All of the major drugs we had focused upon—Zyprexa, Seroquel, Zyvox, and Geodon—were and are still on the market. I would try once again to take on a pharmaceutical giant in court, this time to exact justice beyond a monetary settlement. Most important, I wanted to expose the depth of the betrayal: from the executives who wrote the marketing playbook to the pandering physicians, media conglomerates, and other paid shills who marketed the drugs. Maybe I could also upset the FDA's partnerships with those corporations they were charged, but failed, to regulate.

Foremost on my radar, since going at Eli Lilly, was Johnson & Johnson (J&J), whom we knew had fraudulently marketed its blockbuster antipsychotic Risperdal off-label to nonschizophrenics. Not only had our whistleblower drug reps told us about J&J's off-label marketing schemes, but former J&J employees had also agreed to act as expert witnesses. The challenge would be in framing our case in such a way as to expose the greater picture of how J&J, the largest health product manufacturer in the world, and its Janssen subsidiary, the maker of Risperdal and Invega, had gained off-label market share. Drug reps took their marching orders from the top.

Among the active and former J&J drug reps to speak to us was Victoria Starr, who is as fine and brave a young woman as I've had the pleasure to represent. A second generation pharmacist, with a degree from Washington State University, Vicki had begun her career as an Eli Lilly sales rep based in Portland, Oregon. She made the jump to J&J's Janssen subsidiary in 2001, where, at age 30, she believed she would make greater use of her extensive pharmacology expertise.

Quick to laugh as she is to cry, Vicki had a rude awakening when she entered the Janssen training program. She was not expected to sell Risperdal using technical arguments. Rather, she was encouraged to make generalizations that would induce pediatricians and others to prescribe the drug off-label. Risperdal, she was to tell prescribers, could be used to calm upset children. Physicians had only to lower the adult dosage. Never mind that the drug hadn't been approved for children and that no studies, to her knowledge, had been conducted. "Marketing to kids was the priority," she said. "That was where the company saw the future growth."

Surprise turned to concern when doctors began complaining to Starr about some of the negative side effects their patients were experiencing. Among those side effects was extreme weight gain. Patients could put on as much as a hundred pounds in a matter of months. This was especially alarming because the number of negative side-effects being reported were not what was reflected in the sales literature. There was a disconnect between what she was seeing in the field and what the company was telling her.

When Starr raised questions with her superiors, she was told to downplay the issues. She was also provided with sales brochures which she could leave behind with physicians. These sales materials didn't focus on schizophrenia—which was what the drug had been intended to treat. The emphasis was on using it off-label to treat a "full spectrum" of symptoms that included just about all mental health conditions. Among the photos on these brochures was that of a young girl playing a violin, what drug reps later referred to as the "Yo-Yo Ma" brochure. This image, and others, suggested that the most high-functioning child could safely use the drug without mental impairment.

After two years selling Risperdal, and seeing the children of family friends as young as three being put on the medication, she had had enough. Upset, she called Hector Rosado, a friend from her days with Eli Lilly. Unbeknown to Vicki at the time, Rosado was working with us on our Zyprexa case. Rather than helping her get a job at Lilly, which had been her intention, he recommended that she become one of our *qui tam* whistleblowers. "Call Sheller," he told her.

What a story Starr had to share with us! In the days and months to come, our confidence in what she had to tell us about J&J's marketing to children and other sales practices only increased, and would later be reinforced when we eventually received, though the discovery process, subpoenaed pharmaceutical company brochures, interoffice strategy memos, and office manuals. Along with her testimony, these materials would go a long way toward making our case. This, however, was just the start of her work for us. After she had finally had enough of J&J, and in early 2004 quit her job, she once again encountered the dark side of the pharmaceutical giant.

While working in a senior position with a company managing nursing home pharmacies in the Portland area, and waiting, like James Wetta before her, for government prosecutors to make public our *qui tam* suit, she was repeatedly approached to prescribe the drug to seniors suffering from anxiety and dementia. Forget about the high-functioning school-girl with the violin. The J&J pitch now was how cost-effective Risperdal was. This was because nursing home labor costs could be reduced by keeping patients in a Risperdal chemical straightjacket. "They will sleep all night," the drug reps told her, failing to emphasize, of course, potential negative side effects that included death, diminished mental capacity, and increased risk of diabetes, heart attack, and seizure.

Not long into her new job, Starr was invited to a three-day elder-care seminar in San Francisco in which J&J was sponsoring an informational breakfast devoted to using Risperdal. She didn't just attend the breakfast on our behalf to take notes. With help from federal agents she wore a remote transmitter under her blouse and recorded what was said.

Despite fears that she would be caught, and how her many friends and colleagues in the pharmaceutical industry might later view her actions, she eventually became the key witness and name plaintiff in our *qui tam* Risperdal suit, which we filed in April 2004.

"I had to do what was morally right," she told us. "My conscience wouldn't let me do otherwise."

Among other reps to come on board as our case developed was Judy Doetterl, who had worked for J&J for three years. She, like Starr, was tasked with selling Risperdal off-label. She too wore a hidden transmitter to record marketing presentations.

In addition to sales reps, one of J&J's regional business directors, Kurtis J. Barry, also joined our whistleblower team. What would make his testimony so important was his executive position in the J&J hierarchy; from 1996 to 2009 he was the Risperdal product director and oversaw 60 sales reps and six managers. There was no question, so far as Barry was concerned, who orchestrated the marketing schemes. "The decision to market, promote and sell Risperdal for off-label purposes to the elderly population was made affirmatively and deliberately by defendants' executive and management personnel, and carried out under their authority and direction," he told us.

One of our highest profile witnesses to come forward in the personal injury cases was Tone Jones, the former Oklahoma State quarterback, who had signed on with Janssen in 1998 and eventually became a marketing executive. Among the many other things he had to tell us about Risperdal marketing practices was the inducements that J&J paid to physicians to prescribe the drug to children from 1998 through 2006. Inducements included cash kickbacks, along with a full range of marketing promotions such as all-expenses-paid trips to golfing resorts, admittance to seminars, and meals at exclusive restaurants.

Jones also added items to our list of prescriber inducements that at first seemed the stuff of a Hollywood parody, but proved to be true: drinks at strip clubs, promotional giveaways such as bags of microwave popcorn and brightly colored play toys sporting the Risperdal logo. I expected such incentives from J&J's competitors, but these practices were shameless in that J&J wasn't only in the pharmaceutical business; J&J had earned its century-old reputation selling Band-Aids, baby shampoo, talcum powder, and beauty products.

CHAPTER 8

Politicians, Physicians, and Pharmacists on the Pharma Payroll

ONE OF THE MOST PRESSING questions we had begun asking ourselves about the marketing of Risperdal and the many other antipsychotics was how major pharmaceutical corporations such as J&J had gotten away with what we deemed to be overt criminal behavior. As we knew from back in the years we first took on Eli Lilly, the public had, for want of a better term, been "Bushwacked." By this I don't mean a bird in the bush, but George W. Bush.

This was the substance of testimony from Allen Jones, a whistleblower who came to talk to us, but who ultimately pursued his own case in state court. I share his story here because its speaks to the influence that J&J wielded, and still wields, over our government officials.

Jones, a graduate of Penn State University, was working in the Pennsylvania Office of the Inspector General in 2002 when he was asked to investigate the state's chief pharmacist, Steve Fiorello, who was reported to be managing a private bank account where he deposited checks from pharmaceutical manufacturers. Jones confirmed that this was indeed the case: Fiorello was depositing checks from several drug makers, most notably payments from J&J and its Janssen subsidiary, for traveling and speaking fees, despite the fact that government employees are not allowed to charge for their services or keep honoraria.

Jones didn't, however, stop his investigation here. After further inquiry, he revealed that money was flowing out of Fiorello's account into another government employee's account, that of the director of the Texas Department of Mental Health and Mental Retardation. Additionally, J&J and its Janssen subsidiary were paying for state officials to travel the United States to promote the Texas Medication Algorithm Project (TMAP).

TMAP was purported to help public health officials diagnose mental illness and match patients with appropriate medications and treatment plans. Previous testing of the program had been much heralded by then governor George W. Bush, who had touted the program as a significant time-and-cost-saving diagnostic tool for state public health officials.

As President, Bush initiated the New Freedom Commission on Mental Health (it always intrigued me how the forty-third president would often add the word "freedom" to somehow make some of his more onerous acts and legislative enactments more appealing), which encouraged all states to use the program and fostered legislation that, if enacted, would make TMAP testing mandatory in public schools, publicly funded hospitals, prisons, and other institutions. Pennsylvania was among the state governments that considered buying the program, which was how Fiorello figured into the equation. J&J had provided him funds to attend a TMAP sales conference in New Orleans.

Through interviews with physicians and drug reps, Jones discovered that TMAP was an off-label marketing program funded by drug companies to promote their products. Patients filled out a questionnaire that would be fed into the TMAP program, which in turn identified at-risk individuals and recommended a particular drug and treatment plan for them. The sales literature didn't reveal, however, the Trojan horse rooted deep within the program. By signing on to the TMAP program, all patients determined to be at risk were automatically given one of the new atypical antipsychotics, invariably one produced by a company that had helped to fund the program's development and testing. There were no holistic or nonpharmaceutical options. The only flexibility was what drug was to be prescribed.

More insidious still was the way that the drug manufacturers had found to avoid overtly marketing their drugs for unapproved uses. The TMAP program did it for them without drug companies themselves having to make claims contrary to FDA guidelines. An extreme but true example of how the system worked is a five-year-old in a trial TMAP program in a Texas elementary school who was diagnosed as suffering from obsessive compulsive disorder (OCD) and prescribed Risperdal. Her stunned parents demanded to see the questionnaire she had filled out. The behavior that had triggered the diagnosis turned out to be nothing more than a compulsion to tidy her bedroom—a condition that, according to TMAP, mandated her being given a drug for schizophrenia.

Jones followed an ever-widening money trail. TMAP's so-called independent advisors were on the pharmaceutical industry payroll. Among them was Dr. Steven Shon, the medical director of the Texas Department of Mental Health and Mental Retardation. He had signed undisclosed consulting agreements with Janssen that had given him nearly $50,000 to promote TMAP to Pennsylvania and other states. It should be noted, given what our team would later discover about J&J's promotional undertakings, that the receipt of an honorarium by a public employee who acts in his official capacity is not a misdemeanor but a felony. Such an exorbitant payment to Shon, and so many others, suggests far more than reimbursements covering out-of-pocket expenses.

When Jones submitted his preliminary report to his superior, he was ordered to stop investigating. "Stay away from the drug companies and stay away from TMAP," he was told. From how high up that order came he didn't know, but his instructions were clear. He was to walk away from the investigation. The payments Fiorello was taking were described to him as a state-related personnel issue and nothing more.

When Jones refused to turn his back on the case, he was demoted and replaced as lead investigator. In turn, the case became a misdemeanor offense. Fiorello had breached accepted protocol and had to forfeit honorariums paid to him. Meanwhile, the state of Pennsylvania moved ahead in 2003 to adopt the TMAP program, which was called PennMAP, and it looked like the rest of the country would also fall in line because President Bush had put together a health commission that was promoting it.

According to the Bush commissioners, children of all ages, including preschoolers, needed screening. As stated in their report, testing of many millions of adolescents was necessary because "each year, young children are expelled from preschools and childcare facilities for severely disruptive behaviors and emotional disorders."[xxxvi] Antipsychotics were apparently the answer.

Frustrated that his TMAP findings had been dismissed by his superiors, Jones packed two file boxes of evidence of pharmaceutical companies' bribery and filed a retaliation lawsuit against his former employers and, in 2006, joined the Texas attorney general to file a state False Claims Act case. As he later told a jury, he felt that patients who were automatically switched to drugs such as Risperdal were "being betrayed by the people who were supposed to taking care of them."[xxxvii]

One would naturally think that once such revelations as TMAP became public information that corporate sponsorships of this kind would be held to greater scrutiny. I'm sorry to say that this is not the case. Such popular so-called "independent" health websites as WebMD are doing exactly what TMAP first pioneered, only they continue to get away with it.

As first reported by CBS with a follow-up by the *Washington Post*, no matter which of the 10 answers a web user chose on WebMD's online test for depression, the result came out the same: "You may be at risk for major depression." The suggested remedy, of course, was to discuss your options (medication) with a physician. [xxxviii]

More troublesome still is what viewers aren't told about this and other sites owned by WebMD, which include Drugs. com, MedicineNet, RxList, and theHeart.org.[xxxix] The WebMD depression test was sponsored by Eli Lilly, the maker of anti-depression drug Cymbalta. Further, WebMD's investors include chemical giant DuPont and Rupert Murdoch's News Corp (including his Fox TV networks). Even Monsanto, proponent of GMO's, has joined the act.[xl] What completes these conflicts of interest and blurs the line between ads and independent content is the company's partnership with the FDA.[xli] But that's a story for another book.

CHAPTER 9

Following the Money

WELL IN ADVANCE OF OUR bringing suit, we knew that J&J had resorted to using the same type of media campaigns to sell its product as had Lilly and AstraZeneca. Excerpta Medica, a medical communications agency serving the pharmaceutical industry, had been hired by J&J to ghostwrite and present its pharmaceutical drugs in the best possible light and would also be named in our suit. They had been paid to saturate medical journals with positive stories heralding the release of Risperdal, which, in my opinion, was little more than advertising to push the drug off-label. More than twenty articles appeared in psychiatric journals and medical publications touting Risperdal as the equal of all the new atypical antipsychotics. Physicians took notice and, as J&J's message reached the mainstream media, so did parents of at-risk children.

Even the *New York Times* went on record in Risperdal's support when it quoted Janssen's clinical research director,

Richard Meibach[xlii], as claiming that the drug had "no major side effects," understating the dangers of this drug. As the *Washington Post* reported, the drug supposedly did not cause sleepiness, blurred vision, impaired memory, muscle stiffness, or the many negative side effects commonly associated with the previous generation of antipsychotics. The fact that it might cause diabetes, manic behavior leading to suicide, and the myriad of other conditions we knew came hand in hand with the other atypical antipsychotics was not referenced on the label but buried in small print on the package insert. In one advertisement, which Janssen ran in the *American Journal of Psychiatry*, the company went so far as to claim the drug was as harmless as a placebo.[xliii]

We also knew or at least suspected that the drug studies J&J had used to win FDA approval were rigged, just as we had seen when other dangerous drugs had sped through the approval process. The 1993 study that had won approval for Risperdal had compared multiple low doses of Risperdal with a single high dose of Haldol, the previous generation's antipsychotic. By lowering the intended dosage of Risperdal and upping the normal dosage of Haldol, J&J could be relatively certain of Risperdal's having a good safety profile in comparison. Even the FDA's reviewers, we were told, noted that J&J's studies were incapable of providing any meaningful comparison of the two drugs, and according to one of our whistleblowers, the FDA had warned J&J specifically to not make claims that its drug was any more effective or superior to what had come before it. Yet the FDA granted approval and fast-tracked Risperdal onto the market.

Was the FDA being managed like the doctors had been? Were we seeing hard evidence of the Big Pharma alumni club in action? We had only to look more closely at FDA records and then follow the money to unravel the truth.

Though the agency's stated goal in this new era of "reform" was to streamline the regulatory process to make it more efficient, rigorous, and transparent, the deliberations over Risperdal were carried out in private, without disclosure of scientific data or a public discussion. All we knew for certain, from the official record, was that on April 19, 2004, the FDA sent a warning letter to Janssen. In the FDA's own words, Janssen "misleadingly omits material information about Risperdal, minimizes potentially fatal risks associated with the drug, and claims superior safety... without adequate substantiation." [xliv] From what we were told, no credible evidence of a clinical benefit had ever actually been presented to the FDA by independent, non-industry generated studies to offset what we assumed was evidence of the debilitating and disabling adverse effects of all atypical antipsychotics. Now, it seemed even more outrageous that the FDA had gone ahead and approved the drug. What was going on?

Careful review of the documents brought much more to our attention. Most curiously, the FDA had issued the Risperdal marketing license *after* the company withdrew its application in England, where the British FDA equivalent had determined that safety problems necessitated strengthening restrictions before conditional approval for short-term treatment of manic behaviors could be granted. The drug had not won pediatric approval in Canada for similar reasons.

Shouldn't those concerns have compelled the FDA to be especially conservative and cautious before proceeding? Serious questions were also raised about the FDA's 2006 approval of prescribing Risperdal to autistic children for whom the drug would have little or no obvious benefit except to reduce aggressive tendencies by drugging them to sleep or impairing their mental processes to the point where they acted as if they were asleep. Common sense told us the drug might have profound negative side effects.

Risperdal's success obviously had nothing to do with efficacy but with consensus building and what we soon learned were very well-paid psychiatrists. According to our whistleblowers, foremost among them Dr. Joseph Biederman, a name we were, sadly, all too familiar with. His "research" had sanctioned the dosing of millions of children with harmful, adult psychotropic drugs. Among his victims were seven-year-old Gabriel Myers, four-year-old Rebecca Riley, and toddler Destiny Hager.

Biederman, a Harvard medical professor and Massachusetts General Hospital researcher, was ranked as the scientist with the most-cited ADHD research in the world.[xlv] He led studies examining the prevalence of bipolar disorders in children and almost single-handedly redefined the practice of classifying all mental disorders in children. He did this by conducting studies that purported to show that a substantial minority of children diagnosed with ADHD actually had pediatric bipolar disorder.

In one much heralded study, Biederman reported that nearly a quarter of the children he was treating for ADHD also met his criteria for bipolar disorder and should, therefore, be prescribed antipsychotics. Prior to his study, such a diagnosis was only reserved for older teens and adults who had undergone periods of depression interspersed with dramatic episodes of manic behavior. Biederman changed the playing field by offering a definition of bipolar behavior that consisted entirely of irritability and mood swings, which in essence gave psychiatrists a license to treat virtually all children with antipsychotics.

Hence, when it came to prescribing these drugs, the line between Bipolar I and Bipolar II became largely blurred, and this despite significant medical differences. All patients seemingly became eligible to take the drugs, and the results speak for themselves. Between 1994 and 2003, pediatric bipolar diagnosis went up 4,000 percent in this country.[xlvi]

Thanks to Biederman, many conditions could conceivably fall under the broad canopy of bipolar behavior, including depression, ADHD, and ADD—these are diagnoses I very well could have qualified for in my youth if such conditions had been given a name back then. One of the latest additions to the diagnostic lexicon is oppositional defiant disorder or ODD, which describes youths who often argue with adults, lose their tempers, and are angry, resentful, and easily annoyed by others. What this new diagnosis did, in essence, was to turbocharge what can only be described as pharmageddon.

I knew about Biederman from our previous suits, but we weren't aware of the degree to which he was on the Big Pharma payroll. Few of his colleagues or anyone beside the pharmaceutical executives did. We discovered that between 2000 and 2007, he had received upward of $1.6 million in speaking and consulting fees for promoting drugs to treat the same disorders that he could be credited personally for redefining. He had failed to report this outside income to Harvard. Moreover, J&J paid Biederman $700,000 to underwrite a research center that was devoted to testing and promoting Risperdal. Based on our extensive investigations, we deduced that he had helped J&J coordinate a massive program of deception that won the support of thousands of fellow child psychiatrists.

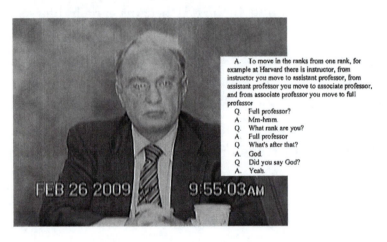

A. To move in the ranks from one rank, for example at Harvard there is instructor, from instructor you move to assistant professor, from assistant professor you move to associate professor, and from associate professor you move to full professor
Q. Full professor?
A. Mm-hmm.
Q. What rank are you?
A. Full professor
Q. What's after that?
A. God.
Q. Did you say God?
A. Yeah.

I would have enjoyed cross-examining Biederman on the witness stand. Thanks in small part to what we uncovered about his ties to J&J, the US Senate investigation got there before me. Rather than being embarrassed by obvious conflicts of interest, Biederman arrogantly lauded the service he was doing for child psychiatry. He compared his work on bipolar disorder to such scientific breakthroughs as the first vaccinations and castigated his critics by saying they weren't on as esteemed a level as he.

When questioned by a colleague of mine on this point, Biederman recited his credentials, highlighting his status as a full professor at Harvard. My colleague then asked him what, if anything, was on a higher level than a fully accredited Harvard medical professor. Biederman declared, in no uncertain terms, "God."[xlvii]

The appearance of so much misbehavior, along with the company's deep pockets, made J&J an obvious target for litigation, and the initial wave of suits focused, as we expected, on claims that J&J had hid or misrepresented studies showing that Risperdal caused diabetes, affected sexual development, and had other negative side effects. I knew better than anyone else that a strong case could be made along these lines, but I was also certain that by focusing on conditions such as diabetes, J&J would argue, truthfully, that people with bipolar and other manic disorders were more likely to suffer from diabetes than the general population. Proving a connection that an individual's condition was a result of the drugs would be extremely difficult.

One of the things I couldn't understand was why J&J's marketing arm had tried so hard to convince physicians that Risperdal was no better or worse than any of the other antipsychotics on the market. Janssen's 2003 marketing plan had actually stated as fact that Risperdal was the same as the other antipsychotics. This was a curious thing to put in a sales plan considering that every drug company I had encountered so far claimed that its product was better than its competitors' or, at the least, stood out because of its value for the cost. This might seem a rather insignificant point but, for someone so steeped in the finer points of pharmaceutical company behavior, it was cause to stop and wonder. Why had J&J and Janssen actively pursued a multimillion-dollar marketing campaign to downplay what made its drug different?

When I began to see Risperdal's effects on the bodies of young men who had used the drug, the answer would become abundantly clear.

CHAPTER 10

Boys Who Grow Breasts

In August of 2005, young A. C. came to see me. He and his parents swore to me that Risperdal had made him grow breasts. He wasn't referring to a modestly enlarged bustline but adult female D cups. More than several hundred children and men would tell me the same thing. Others would grow only one large breast, creating an even more uncomfortable social stigma. In many cases, their breasts would express milk similar to women after giving birth. As insurance defined their condition as cosmetic and didn't cover the mastectomy, only the fortunate few whose parents had enough money could have the unwanted breasts removed. But even then, there were several cases when the removed breasts began growing back before the surgical wounds had even healed. It was as if the victims' brains and hormones had been permanently rewired.

I don't know what horrified me the most, that a drug commonly prescribed for ADD, ADHD, and ODD could disfigure a young boy already struggling to fit in or that children were exposed to this possible side effect by a drug that there was no legitimate reason for them to be taking in the first place. Did J&J's famous credo, dating from 1943, that the company owed its first responsibility to the mothers and fathers, doctors, nurses, and patients who use its products mean nothing?

Based on what I was seeing, I went looking for information connecting Risperdal with increased breast growth. Buried in small print on page seventeen of the Risperdal package insert under "Adverse Reactions" and the heading "Use In Special Populations," I found a single word in a very long list of disclosed potential negative side effects: gynecomastia. In more than three decades of reading lengthy lists of possible side effects, I hadn't before encountered the word and had to consult my medical dictionary to make the connection. Gynecomastia means abnormal breast growth in males (and sometimes females as well) and is attributed, among other things, to increased levels of the hormone prolactin, which stimulates breast growth and milk production.

If I didn't know what gynecomastia meant, I had no reason to believe that parents of children prescribed Risperdal knew what it meant either. My guess was that the vast majority hadn't even read the insert but had relied on their physicians to tell them what side effects they might encounter when taking the drug. Further, I suspected that the reason the side effect hadn't been featured more prominently in the literature was that the effects of Risperdal were more masked in adults than in children. The condition may slip by unnoticed. As it was, the warning that was listed fell under the category of "Special Population," never mind the fact that children and young adults represented the largest proportion of Risperdal's "Special Population" off-label users. The company warned about weight gain but failed to mention that boys and young men could develop breasts and wind up needing bras or having a mastectomy. They were the ones whose lives would seriously change because of Risperdal.

HIGHLIGHTS OF PRESCRIBING INFORMATION
These highlights do not include all the information needed to use RISPERDAL® safely and effectively. See full prescribing information for RISPERDAL®.
RISPERDAL® (risperidone) tablets, for oral use
RISPERDAL® (risperidone) oral solution
RISPERDAL® M-TAB® (risperidone) orally disintegrating tablets
Initial U.S. Approval: 1993

WARNING: INCREASED MORTALITY IN ELDERLY PATIENTS WITH DEMENTIA-RELATED PSYCHOSIS
See full prescribing information for complete boxed warning.
•Elderly patients with dementia-related psychosis treated with antipsychotic drugs are at an increased risk of death.
•RISPERDAL® is not approved for use in patients with dementia-related psychosis. (5.1)

------------RECENT MAJOR CHANGES------------
Warnings and Precautions, Metabolic Changes (5.5)   September 2011

------------INDICATIONS AND USAGE------------
RISPERDAL® is an atypical antipsychotic indicated for:
• Treatment of schizophrenia (1.1)
• As monotherapy or adjunctive therapy with lithium or valproate, for the treatment of acute manic or mixed episodes associated with Bipolar I Disorder (1.2)
• Treatment of irritability associated with autistic disorder (1.3)

------------DOSAGE AND ADMINISTRATION------------
• Recommended daily dosage:

------------CONTRAINDICATIONS------------
• Known hypersensitivity to RISPERDAL® (4)

------------WARNINGS AND PRECAUTIONS------------
• Cerebrovascular events, including stroke, in elderly patients with dementia-related psychosis: RISPERDAL® is not approved for use in patients with dementia-related psychosis. (5.2)
• Neuroleptic Malignant Syndrome: Manage with immediate discontinuation of RISPERDAL® and close monitoring. (5.3)
• Tardive dyskinesia: Consider discontinuing RISPERDAL® if clinically indicated. (5.4)
• Metabolic Changes: Atypical antipsychotic drugs have been associated with metabolic changes that may increase cardiovascular/cerebrovascular risk. These metabolic changes include hyperglycemia, dyslipidemia, and weight gain. (5.5)
  o *Hyperglycemia and Diabetes Mellitus:* Monitor patients for symptoms of hyperglycemia including polydipsia, polyuria, polyphagia, and weakness. Monitor glucose regularly in patients with diabetes or at risk for diabetes. (5.5)
  o *Dyslipidemia:* Undesirable alterations have been observed in patients treated with atypical antipsychotics. (5.5)
  o *Weight Gain:* Significant weight gain has been reported. Monitor weight gain. (5.5)
• Hyperprolactinemia: Prolactin elevations occur and persist during chronic administration. (5.6)
• Orthostatic hypotension: For patients at risk, consider a lower starting dose and slower titration. (5.7)
• Leukopenia, Neutropenia, and Agranulocytosis: Perform complete blood counts in patients with a history of clinically significant low white blood

In clinical trials in 1885 children and adolescents, galactorrhea was reported in 0.8% of RISPERDAL®-treated patients and gynecomastia was reported in 2.3% of RISPERDAL®-treated patients.

Bipolar mania: Adults (2.2)	2 to 3 mg	1 to 6 mg	1 to 6 mg
Bipolar mania: in children and adolescents (2.2)	0.5 mg	1 to 2.5 mg	1 to 6 mg
Irritability associated with autistic disorder (2.3)	0.25 mg (Weight < 20 kg) 0.5 mg (Weight ≥20 kg)	0.5 mg (<20 kg) 1 mg (≥20 kg)	0.5 to 3 mg

• Severe Renal or Hepatic Impairment in Adults: Use a lower starting dose of 0.5 mg twice daily. May increase to dosages above 1.5 mg twice daily at intervals of at least one week. (2.4)
• Oral Solution: Can be administered directly from calibrated pipette or mixed with beverage (water, coffee, orange juice, or low-fat milk. (2.6)
• M-TAB Orally Disintegrating Tablets: Open the blister only when ready to administer, and immediately place tablet under tongue. Can be swallowed with or without liquid. (2.7)

------------DOSAGE FORMS AND STRENGTHS------------
• Tablets: 0.25 mg, 0.5 mg, 1 mg, 2 mg, 3 mg, and 4 mg (3)
• Oral solution: 1 mg per mL (3)
• Orally disintegrating tablets: 0.5 mg, 1 mg, 2 mg, 3 mg, and 4 mg (3)

------------ADVERSE REACTIONS------------
The most common adverse reactions in clinical trials (≥5% and twice placebo) were parkinsonism, akathisia, dystonia, tremor, sedation, dizziness, anxiety, blurred vision, nausea, vomiting, upper abdominal pain, stomach discomfort, dyspepsia, diarrhea, salivary hypersecretion, constipation, dry mouth, increased appetite, increased weight, fatigue, rash, nasal congestion, upper respiratory tract infection, nasopharyngitis, and pharyngolaryngeal pain. (6)
To report SUSPECTED ADVERSE REACTIONS, contact Janssen Pharmaceuticals, Inc. at 1-800-JANSSEN (1-800-526-7736) or FDA at 1-800-FDA-1088 or www.fda.gov/medwatch

------------DRUG INTERACTIONS------------
• Carbamazepine and other enzyme inducers decrease plasma concentrations of risperidone. Increase the RISPERDAL® dose up to double the patient's usual dose. Titrate slowly. (7.1)
• Fluoxetine, paroxetine, and other CYP 2D6 enzyme inhibitors increase plasma concentrations of risperidone. Reduce the initial dose. Do not exceed a final dose of 8 mg per day of RISPERDAL®. (7.1)

------------USE IN SPECIFIC POPULATIONS------------
• Pregnancy: Based on animal data, may cause fetal harm. (8.1)
• Nursing Mothers: Discontinue drug or nursing, taking into consideration the importance of drug to the mother. (8.3)

See 17 for PATIENT COUNSELING INFORMATION

Revised: MM/YYYY

The labeling was also a problem for prescribing physicians. A doctor reading the product insert would have no reason for concern about gynecomastia because the insert listed the condition as a "clinically irrelevant" (meaning less than one in a one thousand) and rare side effect. In other words, breast growth was considered so rare that a risk aversion couldn't be calculated. This wasn't, however, what I was seeing by the number of boys coming into my office. I only had to call a few physicians to connect Risperdal with gynecomastia in a clinically significant way. Surely someone in the pharmaceutical behemoth that was J&J had noticed too.

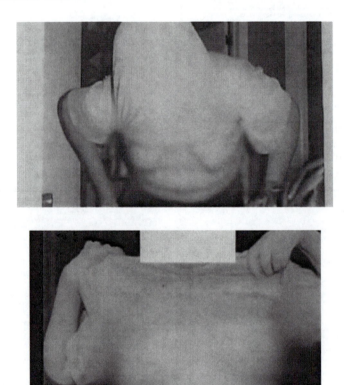

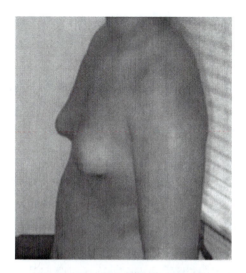

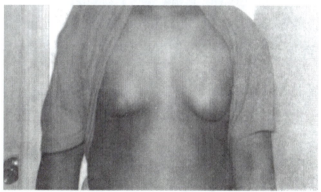

The more people I interviewed, the more upset I became. As I would discover, the nightmare for young gynecomastia sufferers is both physical and psychological. It can begin with taunting on the playground at school. You know the kind: "He's got girl boobs!" or "The fairy queen needs a bra!" This inevitably leads to withdrawal from the public, and for boys going through puberty, it invariably results in gender crises. They start looking more like their mothers than their fathers. Most young boys can't understand what's happening to them. In several notable cases I investigated, adolescents took their own lives. Parents too suffered shame as they blamed themselves for allowing their children to take the drug and, in instances when they could not afford cosmetic liposuction or a mastectomy, were powerless to help.

At the very least, the entire family was traumatized. This was the case of my clients Philip and Benita Pledger and their son, Austin. They asked me to use their names in my book so their personal story can be a lesson to others. One of the reasons is because their son, Austin, is autistic. His challenges began years before his mother and father had ever heard of Risperdal.

The Pledgers are from a small town in rural Alabama and live in a double-wide trailer. They had been trying to have children for twelve years and were considering adoption when Austin, their miracle child, was born to them. By the time Austin celebrated his second birthday, it was clear that he was autistic. He avoided making eye contact. Nor did he pick up on the facial expressions of others. Gradually, other challenges came along. Periodically throughout the day, he would suddenly clap his hands and shout or fly into a rage and beat his head on a table or the floor. Occasionally, he would pinch or bite himself or whomever was closest to him. But despite these hurdles, he was able to attend school and live a relatively normal life. This was made possible by the care and attention he was given by his parents, teachers, classmates, and the greater community of concerned and loving people around Austin. They were his extended family.

Austin Pledger

Risperdal was prescribed at the recommendation of a University of Alabama neurologist when Austin was seven years old. The physician thought it could help. Though the drug was only approved for treating symptoms of schizophrenia in adults, the physician believed it would be soon be approved for other uses and could be especially helpful for autistic children. At least, this is what he had been told by Janssen drug reps, who it was later revealed had visited his office twenty or more times over a two-year period. No mention was made of gynecomastia. Nor was there a black-box warning on the label. Bonita and her husband had no idea that taking a mood-stabilizing pill could possibly cause her son to grow breasts.

Philip and Benita were hesitant to put Austin on Risperdal or any other drug because their situation was manageable. However, if medication could safely help to calm Austin, it would be easier for everyone. "I had never given him any medicine before," Benita, an extremely caring parent and intelligent woman, told us. "So I was nervous about it. I wanted as much information as I could get."

Besides reading the Risperdal package insert, she called Janssen's 1-800 telephone number to discuss her son's condition and what giving him the drug might do. She got an answering machine and, several weeks later, a form letter that failed to address any of her specific questions.

Risperdal seemed to help, but it wasn't the panacea that she and her husband had hoped for. Austin still had emotional eruptions; they just weren't as frequent as they were before taking the drug. Instead of eight to ten daily outbursts, he would have four or five. The problem the Pledgers encountered was their son's incredible weight gain, which began in second grade, when he had been on the drug for a mere two and a half months. By the end of third grade, he had put on nearly fifty pounds. And it was this weight gain that initially kept family members from noticing what was happening to his chest. He was growing breasts.

Rather than taking him off the drug—the Pledgers and their physician still had no idea that Risperdal might have been causing the breast growth—their neurologist added Topamax to what became a three-times-a-day drug cocktail. Topamax, a Janssen Pharmaceutical anticonvulsant approved for epilepsy, was then widely being prescribed off-label for migraines. Drug reps were also pushing it in combination with Risperdal because it allegedly counteracted the weight gain. Other drugs too, which would include Geodon, Abilify, and Prozac, would later be added to the mix in an effort to discover the combination that would be most effective. What Bonita wasn't being told was that each new prescription came with still more side effects.

Austin's condition continued to get worse. He would eventually weigh three hundred pounds and his breasts became 46DD cups. It was quite obvious this was a great embarrassment to him. Benita would often catch Austin looking in the mirror and then crossing his arms in front of his chest and attempting to press his breasts down. As the Pledgers' friends would report, this caring mother, who never cried because her son was autistic, was frequently in tears because of the anguish Austin felt concerning how he looked and at the confusion and disappointment he felt for looking different than other boys and men. On one occasion, when an insensitive teacher mentioned his large breasts in front of him, he smashed them with his hands into the desk top. Continuing at school was out of the question, and Benita had to quit her job to take care of her son. A child already trying to come to grips with the fact that he was somehow different than others was now truly even more different in just about every way.

This, however, was not all. Austin's gynecomastia was permanent.

CHAPTER 11

Risperdal, Prolactin, and the Downstream Effects

TAKING ON J&J OVER THEIR marketing of Risperdal was by no means a new idea as we had already set the example with our pioneering whistleblower litigation with Lilly and AstraZeneca. You might say we had helped to create a cottage industry that had now become the main event in pharmaceutical litigation. As a result, many other attorneys were considering litigation with J&J, and several firms had already filed injury suits. I too would be filing injury suits, in addition to our *qui tam* whistleblower litigation claiming Medicaid and Medicare fraud. However, there were several important legal questions I had to answer before launching a major civil action: How frequently did Risperdal actually result in gynecomastia? How much did J&J and its Janssen subsidiary know and when did they know it?

Based on what we'd discovered, I put the now-considerable resources of our firm into representing more than a hundred civil suits brought on behalf of injured children and their families. As

I'm still trying many of these cases and taking new clients on an almost daily basis, I can only reveal the aspects of our evidence that appeared in public disclosures in cases that have already been settled or where the judge has permitted evidence to be made public.

The vast majority of the evidence we collected was obtained through the discovery process and came directly out of J&J's and Janssen's corporate files along with the records of pharmaceutical industry ghostwriter company Excerpta Medica. This material consisted of 21.7 million pages of correspondence and reports—what's called a "document dump." It's a way that many corporate litigants have of turning over the required documents while obfuscating the truth in an avalanche of irrelevant paperwork. Finding the incriminating evidence was a task that took our team of attorneys and paralegals more than three years. We found more than enough to accomplish what I had set out to do: link corporate executives to a marketing plan to sell a dangerous drug to children—those who stood the most to lose by taking it.

How do I begin to describe the depth of J&J's deceit? My files contain several hundred horror stories of children similar to Austin Pledger who were maimed or disfigured. But the real substance of our case rests in J&J's awareness that this might happen.

Even before drug trials began with human beings, years before Risperdal's release, J&J scientists were reporting that risperidone, the active ingredient of Risperdal and Invega, was causing unusual mammary gland stimulation in rats and dogs. The pharmacological effects were the same in all doses; nerve receptors in the brain were triggering unusually high levels of prolactin. As Risperdal didn't appear to cause other significant negative effects, researchers decided to see what happened in human trials.

The results in human trials were similar to those in the animal studies. After taking a single dose of Risperdal, the volunteers showed prolactin levels increased by 500 to 1,000 percent. Though only short-term testing was done and with few volunteers, one of the test subjects developed a full-blown case of gynecomastia. The scientists conducting the experiment reported this to J&J and debated whether to withdraw the patient from the study. J&J executives responded in writing by saying that due to raised levels of prolactin, such an outcome was possible, but they didn't think gynecomastia was sufficient reason to remove the volunteer from the study. In other words, years before the drug's actual release, J&J admitted that there was a relationship between Risperdal and gynecomastia. J&J had seen it for itself. They also presumably didn't inform the patient or his physician, though this would have been the morally correct action to take. It's also important that executives were made aware that gynecomastia didn't appear to be a negative side effect of the other atypical antipsychotics on the market. Risperdal was somehow different.

A now-public internal memo between J&J executives while Risperdal was still in clinical trials attested to this, but in a different context:

Prolactin elevation with Risperdal has received particular attention due to its receptor-binding affinities. These are different from other atypical antipsychotic agents and can lead to sustained elevated prolactin levels. Symptoms... include gynecomastia.

What was the extent of the risk to potential Risperdal users? J&J did not list gynecomastia as a potential negative side effect on its original package insert in 1993. This came later, in 2003, when J&J admitted that it was a risk but claimed that the condition was so rare that it couldn't even attach an adverse reaction number to the condition. Internal memos between sales reps and the J&J marketing department, however, revealed what wasn't on the packaging.

A training document for sales reps stated that there was a 1 percent risk of developing gynecomastia. The label itself said rare (and remarkably, so does today's label), which is one in a thousand. So the training manual was contrary to what was listed on the labeling. Even this, however, turned out to be a falsehood, as an internal document indicated the real incidence was between 5 and 10 percent.

As we studied the documentation further, we discovered that executives were telling overseas drug regulators what they weren't even telling their own sales reps: regulators were told that the chances of contracting gynecomastia were 4.6 percent. An internal company memo between executives showed the figure to be 6.1 percent, and one of J&J's own studies, which the company did not make public but did show its own sales reps, put the figure at 12.5 percent. If this figure is correct, it means that approximately one or more in every ten males and females exposed to Risperdal could conceivably suffer abnormal breast growth.

This was a serious problem, and the company knew it, which is logically why J&J created a confidential Global Prolactin Task Force. This team of executives and sales reps was led by seasoned drug-marketing guru Gahan Pandina, who was working diligently to understand J&J's liability, what he referred to in correspondence as the "Risperdal, prolactin, and downstream effects." In other words, he was charged with finding out how much the company stood to lose in lawsuits if it kept the drug on the market. There was no forthcoming record from J&J covering this discussion or whether an actual dollar amount had been arrived upon. All that could be concluded from the documents we received was that J&J took a proactive approach. They weren't going to remove the drug from the market but, instead, attempt to steer a course around it.

A 2001 training manual instructed sales reps to lie about the dangers of prolactin increases in the body. They were specifically told to say that changing prolactin levels in the human body was neither good nor bad. The *2003 Risperdal Business Plan* laid out the strategy in greater detail. Under "Promotional Key Issues," the first goal was to show a "lack of differentiation" between Risperdal and J&J's competitors' antipsychotics. In other words, J&J wanted to show that Risperdal was no more dangerous than the other drugs. The plan was to distract prescribing physicians from the real danger while simultaneously feeding them misinformation.

J&J stated this boldly in yet another document that encouraged sales reps to "minimize the risk and importance of prolactin." The goal was to get physicians to believe that (1) Risperdal didn't increase prolactin any more than its competitors, and (2) oh, by the way, prolactin doesn't matter much anyway. Both, in my opinion, were huge lies.

J&J executives also went out of their way to discourage doctors from monitoring the prolactin level in their patients' bloodstreams because it might shed light on what Risperdal was doing. "I would advise against any recommendation regarding monitoring of prolactin," Gahan Pandina was told.

Unfortunately for Risperdal users, J&J went even further than failing to monitor a problem it was well aware of. In an undated internal documented entitled "Now Is the Time to Grow Your Risperdal Market Share," sales reps were instructed to tell prescribers that all of the atypical antipsychotics increase prolactin in the same amount; no one knows whether increased prolactin is good or bad; and that, if there were any concerns, they should add a second drug to a patient's daily antipsychotic cocktail. Remember three-year-old Destiny Hager? She died after taking a combination of Risperdal and eight other drugs.

Such egregious behavior makes one wonder about what other potential side effects prescribers were not told about. As the new Drexel University study on SSRIs has shown, there may be a link between Risperdal and autism.[xlviii] Another study, which has not been made public, is purported to allege that Risperdal and other drugs commonly prescribed to children with ADD and

ADHD shrinks the brain.[xlix] How many more horrendous side effects will be discovered?

There was no question that doctors, nurses, and scientists studying Risperdal had alerted J&J executives to the prolactin problem. This is clear in internal memos and also from a lengthy paper trail of dissatisfied customers, among them a nurse who wrote the following letter to J&J in 2001:

> I am working in an adolescent residential treatment center. We give a lot of Risperdal for aggressive behaviors. While we have been pleased with the decreased negative behaviors, we are seeing a major problem of gynecomastia in the males and lactation among the females because of the increased prolactin levels. Do you have any research regarding this side effect? If taken off Risperdal, will the breasts return to normal size or is this permanent? How high does the prolactin levels have to be before breast development is seen? This is very distressing to the clients, and they are refusing to take the med because of this major side effect...We would appreciate any information or suggestions.

This nurse, who had nothing but the best interests of her patients in mind, simply wanted to know what research J&J had on this condition and whether it was permanent. These were questions J&J did not want to answer. They didn't respond the first time she wrote, or two years later, when she wrote a second letter after learning that J&J sales reps were telling physicians that increased prolactin was nothing to worry about because it was not clinically relevant.

The nurse knew better and so did an upset J&J employee who saw the writing on the wall and wrote, "It seems clear we need to more aggressively own up to prolactin elevation. It's no longer enough to say 'prolactin elevation is not clinically relevant.'"

J&J didn't address the issue except to continue obfuscating the truth. When discussions began about establishing a prolactin help line to handle the growing concerns in the medical community, J&J marketing executive Ronald Kalmeijer told his staff that doing so wouldn't help its bottom line: "Our standpoint is that prolactin-related side effects is a nonissue. Our tactics need to be supportive of that." In follow-up correspondence, he again revealed what was worrying him: "I am not comfortable with sharing so much negative details...I am not comfortable with stating that patients with prolactin-related side effects may benefit from switching [to another drug]."

J&J didn't just kill the hotline; it actively prevented physicians from learning the truth. When a new study showing increased prolactin levels was to be presented at a medical conference, J&J sent executive orders to effectively spin the data. "There are some figures that I think should be deleted," J&J executive Ramy Mahmoud wrote to a physician in charge of preparing the materials for the conference.

Mahmoud got the anticipated response. "I attempted to include only positive data, so that the data cannot be used against us," the physician responded. "I am happy to delete any figures. I am also happy to change any text."

When the National Institute of Mental Health planned a study to compare antipsychotic drugs, one of J&J's chief executives told his colleagues, "I think we have to take this very seriously and capitalize on our knowledge of both Risperdal and competitors, trying to influence as much as we can the protocols in order to be sure we get good results."

When child psychiatrist Dr. Eric Benjamin informed J&J about a Risperdal study he had conducted at Phoenix Children's Hospital, J&J immediately offered help "as to how the study should be written up." Its enthusiasm disappeared when the company received Dr. Benjamin's data on prolactin. Of the thirty-five patients studied, twenty-two gained between five and fifty pounds. The response from Janssen's chief executive said it all: "I would prefer NOT TO TOUCH THIS." For reasons that were not clarified in follow-up correspondence, Dr. Benjamin's study never saw the light of day.

Concern over prolactin increase, however, didn't prevent J&J from flooding the media with upbeat reports. Just as Eli Lilly, AstraZeneca, and Pfizer had done, J&J turned to Excerpta Medica to praise the benefits of their drug. J&J's stated goal, as presented in internal correspondence, was to "redefine how we achieve support for messaging through publications and thereby achieve greater commercial success in the marketplace." Excerpta Medica was paid to "manage the content, direction, and timing of data dissemination to competitive advantage." Before these allegedly impartial articles were even written and the physicians found to affix their names to them as the supposed authors, the contents and objectives of the articles were outlined and the text written by J&J marketing executives.

Where did J&J want its Risperdal articles published? As other documents attested, it wanted Excerpta Medica–generated stories to appear in the publication that would most bolster sales to children: The *Journal of American Academy of Child and Adolescent Psychiatry*—despite the fact that Risperdal had never been approved for use in children.

Excerpta Medica's program was successful. In 2001, journals highlighted Risperdal more than all other drugs combined. By 2003, half of all Risperdal prescriptions were being written for children and the elderly, and 90 percent of those prescriptions were for vague, hard-to-define, and overdiagnosed behavioral conditions like ADD, ADHD, along with mood disorders, such as depression. J&J studiously tracked these sales yet made no effort to inform or warn prescribers of Risperdal's unique dangers.

During the thirteen years that Risperdal was not approved for children, while Dr. Biederman and others were breaking down the diagnostic barriers, J&J made more than $100 million per year selling its drug to children. It made $122 million in sales in 1999 and $178 million in sales in 2000. Still, J&J wanted more. Its plan was to expand sales until Risperdal became its first billion-dollar seller, which it did, peaking at $4.5 billion in 2007, then $3.4 billion in 2008. By 2010, when the drug's patent ran out and it was competing with generic drug makers, the revenue had dropped to $527 million according to J&J's earnings reports.

Internal memos outlined the scheme to increase market share to children. First, they would produce a drug that was administered more easily to youth. Initially produced as an injection or an unpleasant-tasting risperidone solution, the drug was reconfigured as an easy-to-swallow tablet called Quicksolv. In conceiving the new product, J&J advisors wanted to make certain that the tablet tasted good and that managed care insurers would cover the anticipated prescriptions' cost. These were the two primary concerns when Quicksolv went into production.

"I cannot wait for this to come out," one Risperdal-prescribing physician wrote. "We will give this to every kid [in our hospital]."

In anticipation of Quicksolv's release, J&J pumped out publicity for the drug by positing messages for children and adolescents in abstracts, posters, presentations, symposia, and more journal articles. In one of the most morally reprehensible campaigns J&J launched entitled Consequences for Not Treating Children, it warned physicians about what may happen if they didn't prescribe Risperdal to children with behavioral disorders. The document suggested that these children could go on to develop or experience antisocial personality disorder, alcohol and drug abuse, anxiety, depressive symptoms, hospitalization, and criminal behavior that included but was not limited to driving while intoxicated and commissioning violent crimes.

Dr. Biederman was once again called into action. By this time, the challenge was no longer selling Risperdal to children. J&J had already succeeded in doing that. It was obtaining FDA approval for conditions it was already being prescribed for; in other words, increased sales were not the objective. Rather, for new indications or conditions J&J received FDA approval for, its patent could be extended by an additional six months or a year.

Dr. Biederman stepped up his campaign by working aggressively to convince the FDA that Risperdal was safe and effective, and he used his J&J-sponsored research center at Harvard to prove it. However, to be effective, he had to hide his conflict of interest. In one of the documents we uncovered, a J&J executive acknowledged his pleasure at having Biederman on board, noting that he was "not perceived to be aligned with any [pharmaceutical] company in particular" and that his relationship with J&J demonstrated "a clear example of the utility of partnering...[with physicians who have a significant impact upon the field of child and adolescent psychiatry]."

As internal memos also revealed, J&J helped to write the studies that Dr. Biederman presented as his own, though we might never have known if Biederman hadn't taken the trouble to thank J&J's task leader: "Thanks Gahan...If you could help draft the abstract for Tuesday, it will be great."

J&J's tactics were working. By 2005, Risperdal had become J&J's top-selling product, with sales over $3.5 billion, not only raising the company's stock price but also garnering bonuses for its executives. Meanwhile, thousands and perhaps tens of thousands of children and adults were suffering because of it.

As the minutes of an FDA Pediatric Advisory Committee panel meeting makes clear, over thirty people died from taking the drug in 2007, at least eleven of who were children whose Risperdal treatment was unapproved by the FDA. Among them was a nine-year-old girl who had suffered a fatal stroke twelve days after starting Risperdal therapy. Now I fully understand that killing someone with a prescription pill is not the same as killing someone with a bullet, but the end result is the same. Had this advisory committee lost sight of the fact that this drug was not approved for children, or was this business as usual at the FDA?

There were no figures made available to the FDA about how many boys suffered gynecomastia, as purportedly no authoritative studies had been conducted. However, as we now know, at least one study had been conducted, but Janssen researchers had lied about its findings and further mislead or coerced reviewers of their research data into presenting a false public record of what was actually known about the drug.

Even without this vital information, however, the subject of widespread pediatric use of Risperdal caught the attention of the FDA committee tasked to monitor such trends. Nearly four hundred thousand children were being treated with Risperdal and over half these children were twelve years or younger. Adult use was declining by 5 percent while pediatric prescriptions were increasing by 10 percent.

As the session's minutes reported, the committee discussed adverse events related to product use, off-label use including risks and benefits, age subgroups, product labeling, and the effects of long-term use. Twelve of the fourteen-member committee concluded that the current labeling was inadequate. Specifically, they unanimously supported labeling in addition to the standard and ongoing safety monitoring.

The advisory committee recommended the following:

1. Additional follow-up regarding on-label and off-label product use of this class of drug products with specific attention to age and indication the product is being used for.
2. Additional follow-up regarding metabolic syndrome, growth, sexual maturation, and hyperprolactinemia.
3. Studies, which may be collaboratively developed with NIH, on long-term effects in the pediatric population of this class of products.
4. Additional follow-up on extrapyramidal side effects in the pediatric population.
5. Additional evaluation of this class of antipsychotic medications and concomitant drug use.
6. Committee is not recommending any public communication before additional discussion that should occur after receipt of data from above recommendations.

Despite these recommendations, no monitoring appears to have taken place, no health studies were commissioned, and no changes were made to Risperdal's labeling. Dr. Thomas Laughren, who had long been a pivotal member of the FDA's Center for Drug Evaluation and Research (CDER) and who sat in on the committee meeting, had apparently overruled the recommendations. He reported that the FDA could do little to fix the problem of off-label marketing, as this was a matter between the physician and the patient. Medical specialty societies, he said, must do the job of educating doctors about the drug's side effects. "It's not the FDA's primary responsibility."

A year later, the Alliance for Human Research Protection reported that Dr. Laughren, like his colleague Biederman, had maintained close, ongoing collaborative ties with pharmaceutical industry officials and industry-financed psychiatrists in academia and professional associations.[l] He had participated in influential industry-sponsored consensus panels convened by the American Academy of Child and Adolescent Psychiatry (AACAP) that had recommended expanded use of atypical antipsychotics for unapproved, off-label uses in children, and lent his name and position to articles for which research and funding were provided by the very pharmaceutical companies whom he was charged with regulating.[li] True to his values, Laughren left the FDA in late 2012 and became a defense expert for drug companies in litigation.

Fortunately, we didn't have to rely on Dr. Laughren's appraisal of Risperdal to build our case against J&J. Former FDA Commissioner David Kessler wrote a ninety-two-page expert report for submission in our suits. He had many levels of concern:

The promotion of nonapproved uses by a manufacturer, because it undercuts the system and safeguards of drug regulation, is concerning. The promotion of nonapproved uses by a manufacturer of powerful drugs is more concerning. The promotion of nonapproved uses of powerful drugs to the most vulnerable children is most concerning. Janssen's promotion of Risperdal, a powerful drug, for nonapproved uses in the most vulnerable children is deeply troubling...They broke the law.

Kessler was not only willing to submit his report for trial, he was also willing to testify as a "failure to warn" expert. J&J fought the entry of his name onto our list of expert witnesses at every step of the way, and this was after we added a J&J corporate executive to the same list: CEO William Weldon.

I had the most rock-solid case of my career.

CHAPTER 12

Band-Aids, Baby Shampoo, and Big Pharma

IN 2006, AFTER CONDUCTING TWO years of research, we began to file our first hundred individual Risperdal injury cases. As a result of the publicity, over a thousand more Risperdal victims would eventually find their ways to my office. Interestingly, J&J showed no evidence of willingness to discuss the charges—just the opposite. The company prepared for a protracted court battle, fighting us at every step of the judicial process, from our pretrial discovery requests to the expanding number of executives, marketing reps, and Excerpta Medica consultants we wished to depose.

The pressure was on J&J from the start when, on September 2010, a bellwether Risperdal consumer fraud case was launched in Louisiana. The jury came back with an astonishing $257 million judgment. We knew with certainty that the case would be appealed and the settlement likely overturned by a higher court, but a precedent had been set. Three months later, a South Carolina judge upheld a $327 million jury verdict against J&J and Janssen for off-label marketing. Though South Carolina's

Supreme Court would reduce the penalty to $124 million, another precedent was set.

The trickle of suits—both for side effects such as gynecomastia and for off-label marketing—threatened to become a flood tide in 2012, when J&J's longtime CEO William Weldon unexpectedly announced his retirement, which he left for with "parting gifts" of $143.5 million in pension, retirement benefits, and deferred compensation.

My litigation, and that of other attorneys pressing charges, was not cited as the reason, but then again, the press didn't yet know what we and the US attorneys knew. The paper trail of documents that the prosecution were prepared to introduce as evidence ran up the entire chain of J&J command. In what may have been a serious tactical blunder on J&J's part, Weldon was replaced by Alex Gorsky, whose long career with J&J had begun in its Janssen subsidiary. Most important to our cases, he had been VP of marketing at Janssen when it had ramped up Risperdal sales to children. From our point of view, the announcement was almost too good to believe. When our primary cases came to trial, we would call none other than J&J's current CEO to the witness stand.

A month after Gorsky's promotion, another state Risperdal case went to trial in Arkansas. In a state with less than 1 percent of the US population, the jury verdict was for $1.1 billion. The press, which had long reported that a total global settlement would be in the neighborhood of $1 billion, had to recalculate. The new estimate was placed at $2.2 billion.

Another case, with our plaintiff A. B., who suffers from gynecomastia, went to trial in Philadelphia on September 10, 2012, and ended the same day. When we called CEO Alex Gorsky to the witness stand, J&J claimed he was traveling overseas and unavailable to testify, and J&J's PR person said, he had been deposed for seven hours, hence his appearance in court would be unnecessary.

Travel plans notwithstanding, it was clear J&J's plan was to keep Gorsky off the stand, and a judge agreed he did not have to testify. J&J attorneys then asked for a recess to discuss terms of a settlement. Ten days later, our second Pennsylvania case came to trial and ended the same way. On October 4, 2012, we settled four more cases. I can't discuss the dollar amounts in these personal injury cases because, at present, these must be kept confidential. I can, however, reveal the jury award to Austin Pledger, the autistic boy who was put on Risperdal at age eight; he received $2.5 million in compensatory damages.

As satisfying as the results of these trials were and continue to be, nothing could beat the clarion call of November 2013: Attorney General of the United States, Eric Holder, announced that the US attorney's office in Philadelphia had agreed to a historic $2.2 billion settlement with J&J/Janssen for the whistleblower off-label marketing and illegal kickbacks over Risperdal and Invega. The case that we had developed and presented to the US government almost ten years earlier had finally concluded.

Here in our midst was the largest pharmaceutical settlement for a single drug in US history. And though it was US Attorneys General whose faces beamed before national cameras to make the announcement, this was, in essence, our client, our case, and our hard work coming to fruition. It took ten years, yes, but some things take that much time and are worth waiting for.

Did we win?

From a financial point of view, there is no question that J&J has been hit with a staggering federal penalty—a new all-time high for a single drug marketed by a single company. But this penalty is not as significant as I believe it could or should be. Nor will the penalty stop Big Pharma's addiction to off-label sales and the profits. Shares in J&J are today trading at a ten-year high, and its executives receive among the highest bonuses and salaries in any company worldwide. As *Forbes* pointed out when the settlement was announced, "the potential of off-label sales may just be too alluring for drug makers to kick their habit."[lii]

Further, in a disheartening upset that has sadly become the new trend in the conservative higher courts, corporation-friendly Supreme Court Justices in Louisiana and Arkansas have now reversed the lower court's state verdicts against J&J. How the decision makers justified the reversals differs, but in Arkansas, the court interpreted the Arkansas Medicaid Fraud False Claims Act and the Arkansas Deceptive Trade Practices Act (MFFCA) to say that only healthcare facilities can be liable in their state for wrongdoing under the act and that J&J is not a healthcare facility and shouldn't be held accountable. Such an interpretation of the law may be justified, but what of the injured plaintiffs? Does J&J have no responsibility?

A similarly mystifying turn of events occurred in 2014, when Philadelphia Judge Arnold New overturned a previous ruling by deciding that punitive damages—those intended to punish a defendant for conduct or misbehavior—would not be allowed in Risperdal personal injury cases. Judge New's reasoning was that Janssen's headquarters are in New Jersey, and New Jersey's product liability law does not allow punitive damages in claims involving drugs that require premarket FDA approval (which is, no doubt, why Janssen, J&J, and so many other pharmaceutical companies are headquartered there).

Never mind that Risperdal injuries, such as those experienced by Austin Pledger, occurred throughout the United States and that Janssen's previous position was that punitive damages should be based on the law of the state where the drug was marketed, prescribed, and ingested. Also, never mind that Janssen committed fraud by withholding from the FDA clinical trial results linking Risperdal to gynecomastia and that its sales reps were flogging its unapproved-by-the-FDA off-label "benefits" to physicians in contradiction to federal law. Such issues are not to interfere with New Jersey's product liability statutes, so Judge New has declared. (And this, despite a 2015 decision by New's colleague Judge Lawrence Stengle, who reached the opposite conclusion in a case involving fatal liver damage caused by Tylenol.)

Remember also, in regards to our *qui tam* case, that my own state of Pennsylvania is not one of the 29 states that has yet passed a False Claims statute. Hence, Pennsylvania (and 21 other states) will not receive any of our 2.2 billion settlement! Further, it is my understanding that Alan Jones, the Philadelphia investigator who exposed the TMAP super-fraud, and was represented by another law firm, received no whistleblower recompense from his own state. To my mind, that's not justice. It's not even common sense.

There is other sad news to report: no J&J or Janssen executives, or even low-ranking sales reps, will go to jail or be charged with a serious crime. Like its competitors at Eli Lilly, AstraZeneca, and Pfizer, J&J cut a deal: in return for immunity from felony prosecution, the company will pay a criminal fine and plead guilty to one misdemeanor charge only. And this, shamefully, for off-label marketing to the elderly and not children. As I'm not the attorney general, the decision was not mine to make.

The jury is still out on impact our litigation may have on the careers of executives who made the marketing decisions. I do, however, have reason to be modestly hopeful that their reputations have been tarnished, if not by the onerous Risperdal revelations, then by the company's unprecedented product recalls of such J&J staples as Motrin, Rolaids, Tylenol, and Mylanta, and its reformulation of J&J's No More Tears baby shampoo and one hundred other baby products (not to mention Neutrogena soaps and creams) after they were discovered to contain the potentially harmful chemicals formaldehyde and 1,4-dioxane. And that in addition to recalls and litigation over its defective hip implants, injury-inducing vaginal mesh devices, and tendon-snapping, neurologically-damaging Levaquin antibiotic.

A group that has taken the matter into its own hands by demanding change has formed an organization called Boycott the Band-Aid Campaign.[liii] Stockholders have also taken the matter into their hands by launching a suit against ten J&J board members and several executives, including CEO Alex Gorsky and former CEO Bill Weldon. They claim that J&J's corporate directors and executives failed to stop criminal wrongdoing and misrepresentation of its products when they could and should have done so.[liv] Another suit brought by one stockholder alleges a breach of fiduciary duties in connection with the CEO's compensation. The plaintiff claims that Weldon, who reportedly earned a combined $175 million from 2006 until his retirement, was grossly overpaid given the "highly publicized compliance failures, recalls, and misconduct" at J&J.[lv] While J&J's reputation and earnings suffered, its CEO's annual compensation doubled.

Though I am pleased that stockholders and others have finally, if belatedly, woken up to what has been going on at J&J, one can only wonder what was running through the board members' minds when Weldon, who was voted one of the worst CEOs of 2011 by the *New York Times*, was permitted to choose Alex Gorsky—to my mind the most corrupt manager in the company—to take his place. Perhaps I'll get to find out one day if I get to cross-examine him on the witness stand. But I'm not holding my breath. The courts have repeatedly shielded him from cross-examination in this case as well as in another civil action, that one having to do with Exelon, the Alzheimer's drug produced by Novartis, where Gorsky also worked.

I reference the Exelon case because, in my opinion, it reveals a similar pattern of fraud and smoking-gun evidence that executives knew exactly what their marketing departments were up to. Gorsky, who had his start at Janssen as a sales rep and went on to become vice president of marketing and sales and then CEO, left for Novartis in 2004, just after he succeeded in making Risperdal the biggest-selling drug in the company's history. He would work similar magic for Exelon. And similarly, during his tenure, Novartis was accused of making false claims to Medicare and Medicaid for reimbursement of Exelon, was alleged to have violated anti-kickback statutes by rewarding doctors who wrote prescriptions of its drugs, and making misleading risk presentations. Had Gorsky brought his Janssen playbook with him to Novartis?

And what of Dr. Biederman who, to my mind, is just as culpable as Weldon and Gorsky? The Massachusetts General Hospital and Harvard Medical School took a step in the right direction, however small, by disciplining him. As punishment, Biederman and three other physicians must refrain from pharmaceutical industry–sponsored, "outside" activities for one year, and for two years after the ban ends, they must obtain permission from the hospital and Harvard Medical School before engaging in any industry-sponsored or paid outside activities. These physicians were also requested to undergo certain, unspecified training and will also face delays before being considered for promotions or advancements. Perhaps such training will require that Biederman undergo the same mental health testing that he recommended for a generation of children.

This punishment is not to the measure I had hoped or anticipated. Biederman hasn't, for example, been asked to return the more than $1.6 million he earned from pharmaceutical companies for consulting fees. Nor have any efforts been made to rescind the awards for excellence he has received from the American Psychiatric Association or the American Academy of Child and Adolescent Psychiatry. He remains in the Children and Adults with Attention-Deficit/Hyperactivity Disorder (CHADD) Hall of Fame—or should it more appropriately be called the Hall of Shame?

I do, however, have marginally good news from among the fifty so-called independent physician researchers at some two-dozen universities—including Harvard, Johns Hopkins, and Stanford—who participated to varying degrees in helping J&J counter fears that Risperdal shouldn't be prescribed to children. Scientists Denis Daneman and Robert Findling, who, with help from J&J, published a 2003 paper that asserted that Risperdal was safe and should be administered to children in the *Journal of Clinical Psychiatry*, bravely stepped forward to try and right the wrong.[lvi]

Dr. Daneman, a professor and chair of pediatrics at the University of Toronto, said that he would be donating to charity the money he received from J&J for the article and has asked the journal to remove his name from the article. One of the coauthors, Robert Findling, a professor of psychiatry and behavioral sciences at the Johns Hopkins University, indicated that he might do the same. "In light of recent events," Dr. Findling said, "I am concerned about the questions raised, and if there are errors, I am committed to determining what they may be and to correcting them."[lvii]

Their change of heart, however, was not without a courtroom drama. When their analysis became the subject of judicial scrutiny, J&J came to their rescue by offering up a reanalysis of the data upon which they based their arguments. Not surprisingly, the new (or re-imagined) J&J funded research, which they tried to submit in the middle of a trial, was alleged to support their conclusions. Daneman, Findling, and J&J were off the hook, so it seemed. Only they weren't. Under scrutiny and cross-examination, the so-called reanalysis (produced 13 years after the fact) was rejected in December 2015 by the jury, and J&J's study dismissed as the sham we believe it was.[lviii] If anything, the reanalysis actually supported our failure to warn and causation claims and confirmed Dr. Kessler's analysis. Whether or not this means Dr. Daneman will still be sending his check to charity I can't say, but it would be nice if he did. I am not so hopeful for a reordering at the FDA or that Risperdal will either be removed from the market or relabeled, so that physicians and their patients know the real dangers.

In this regard, I took matters into my own hands by filing a citizen's petition with the FDA to revoke approval for Risperdal, Invega, and all related generics until and unless the long-term safety of the product can be demonstrated. To bolster my case, I prepared and submitted to FDA Commissioner Margret

Hamburg a dossier containing copies of the court-permissible documents that outline and support the claims I made and will continue to make in civil court. I further requested that the FDA obtain the court's permission to review the many documents in my possession that are still under court seal or to request copies of these documents directly from J&J.

My petition and the accompanying documents that I am permitted to make public have been posted on my website. Though they represent only a small percentage of the evidence I would like to make public, they are worthy of your close attention. The truth will surprise you.

 1528 Walnut Street, 4ᵗʰ Floor * Philadelphia, PA 19102
215/790-7300 * www.sheller.com

2012 AUG 28 A 9: 46

August 27, 2012

Margaret A. Hamburg, M.D.
Commissioner
Food and Drug Administration
Department of Health and Human Services
WO 2200
10903 New Hampshire Avenue
Silver Spring, MD 20993-0002

Dear Dr. Hamburg,

Sheller, P.C. represents individuals and groups of individuals who have suffered serious physical and mental injuries caused by prescription pharmaceuticals, biologicals and devices. We presently represent hundreds of individuals who have suffered serious harm, including gynecomastia and prolactin-related injuries as a result of their ingestion of the second-generation atypical anti-psychotic medications Risperdal® (risperidone) marketed by Ortho-McNeil-Janssen Pharmaceuticals, Inc., formerly Janssen Pharmaceutical, Inc., a subsidiary of Johnson & Johnson (hereinafter "J&J").

This Petition is an Amendment to our Petition previously filed and docketed at **FDA-2012-P-0857**. The purpose of this Amendment is to demonstrate the manner in which the current Prescribing Information for risperidone actively impedes physicians' ability to comply with the standard of care for the monitoring, diagnosis and treatment of hyperprolactinemia (as described by J&J's own prolactin consultant); and how an adequate warning in this regard would result most if not all adolescents being switched from risperidone one of the many other atypical antipsychotics with a safer prolactin profile.

Unfortunately for all concerned (except perhaps for J&J), after nearly two years waiting for a review of my submissions, Janet Woodcock, director of the FDA's Center for Drug Evaluation and Research, rejected my petition. Rather than demand a long-term clinical study of Risperdal, Invega, and all related generics or order an investigation of the documents I called attention to, the FDA chose instead to rely on J&J's word that it had already submitted all relevant documents, clinical trial tests, and research materials to the FDA and that there was no need for further investigation.

In other words, the FDA wouldn't even review the evidence. Never mind that I was representing many hundreds of children harmed by this drug and that the attorney general had just settled with J&J for $2.2 billion dollars. Why, you might ask, would a company settle for such a monumental penalty if it was not guilty of misbehavior? Wouldn't you imagine that our government's drug regulatory agency would be interested in what the attorney general found?

Unbelievable!

Such actions by the FDA are what prompted nine FDA scientists in 2009 to send President Obama a detailed letter accusing the agency of, among other things, "being fundamentally broken" and stating that there was "well-documented corruption and wrongdoing," that "the scientific review process...has been corrupted and distorted," and that FDA administrators had "ordered, intimidated coerced scientists (into doing their bidding)"; and finally, they urged a "complete change in the FDA's current leadership" as the drug companies were telling the administrators what to do.[lix] How were the scientists who signed this letter received? In 2012, FDA senior management installed spyware on the computers of some or all of these scientists.[lx]

There's a word for what drove the criminal behavior and corruption we uncovered at every step along the way of this case: greed. The greater question is what we are going to do about it collectively.

Afterword
Don't Trust a Felon

I N   L E S S   T H A N   H A L F   A decade, our firm was substantially responsible for four of the top eight Big Pharma whistleblower settlements of all time, a sum exceeding $6 billion.

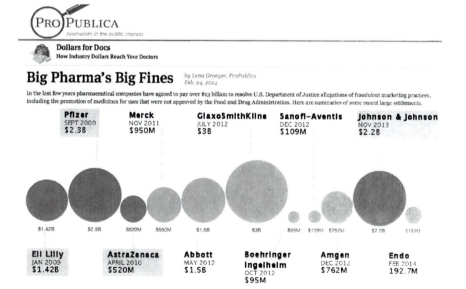

PRO PUBLICA
Journalism in the public interest

Dollars for Docs
How Industry Dollars Reach Your Doctors

Big Pharma's Big Fines
by Lena Groeger, ProPublica
Feb. 24, 2014

In the last few years pharmaceutical companies have agreed to pay over $13 billion to resolve U.S. Department of Justice allegations of fraudulent marketing practices, including the promotion of medicines for uses that were not approved by the Food and Drug Administration. Here are summaries of some recent large settlements.

Pfizer SEPT 2009 $2.3B	**Merck** NOV 2011 $950M	**GlaxoSmithKline** JULY 2012 $3B	**Sanofi–Aventis** DEC 2012 $109M	**Johnson & Johnson** NOV 2013 $2.2B

$1.42B $2.3B $520M $950M $1.5B $3B $95M $109M $762M $2.2B $193M

Eli Lilly JAN 2009 $1.42B	**AstraZeneca** APRIL 2010 $520M	**Abbott** MAY 2012 $1.5B	**Boehringer Ingelheim** OCT 2012 $95M	**Amgen** DEC 2012 $762M	**Endo** FEB 2014 192.7M

However much I would like to celebrate, I can't claim victory. Newer and potentially more lethal pharmaceuticals enter the market each month, and the corporate titans with whom I do battle become ever more powerful and cunning. Drug company executives continue to manipulate test results, ghostwrite reviews of their own products, influence physicians into doing their bidding, and lobby legislators and the judiciary to rolling back initiatives put in place to regulate them, and all the while, the victims of their fraud die or are injured in ever greater numbers. Yet these are the same companies to whom we entrust our health.

The obvious place to begin an overhaul of the system is with the FDA. Our primary pharmaceutical regulatory agency must not continue to be the Big Pharma alumni club, in which pharmaceutical executives go to work for the FDA—oftentimes making regulatory decisions on matters affecting their industry and sometimes even their own companies—and then go back to higher-paying jobs in the drug industry. Lobbyists and lobbying are unnecessary in this equation because there is no middleman between the regulators and the influence peddlers. In fact, the conflict of interest is mandatory: by law, industry representatives have to sit on the FDA's so-called "independent" scientific advisory committees, and FDA administrators must, by law, consult and negotiate with the industry on the agency's goals and plans.

Let's be honest about the conflict of interest and do something about it. A significant moratorium must be put into place on how soon a former FDA employee or scientist can receive funding or be employed in the industry. Better still, let's recruit scientists and administrators whose dedication is to our nation's health, not the industry's bottom line.

Next on my agenda would be producing high-quality clinical trials that the FDA can use to evaluate the safety and efficacy of a new drug. The problem here is that the pharmaceutical companies now conduct, oversee, and subsidize nearly all clinical testing. As we have seen, they select the trial participants, stop testing that would cast their products in an unfavorable light (and bury the evidence that testing even took place), decide who sees the raw data, chooses what findings are submitted to the FDA, and contracts with "opinion leaders" to publish favorable reviews in prestige, high-impact journals. And if being both the judge and jury weren't enough, the clinical trial markers that the FDA uses to determine a drug's efficacy couldn't be any lower. The drug sponsor must only demonstrate that their product is an improvement, however marginal, over taking a placebo, which in essence is doing nothing.

Beyond certain moral issues—such as whether or not human guinea pigs should be paid to participate in corporate-sponsored drug trials—I have no objection to drug companies or any other corporations testing their own products. The more testing the better! To my mind, however, such testing should only be the starting point though—that which the FDA should use to determine a new drug's *eligibility* to begin the approval process. Otherwise, the temptation for Big Pharma to manipulate the evidence is too great. The common-sense next step would be for the FDA to conduct its own third-party, independent testing. The emphasis here would be on health as an inalienable right in our nation, not big businesses where a handful of corporations play puppet master. Rather than working for the pharmaceutical industry—which, in essence, is what the FDA is now doing—it would be working for the American people.

The most suitable candidates to partner with the government would be teaching hospitals, university laboratories, and those we can presume to be less inclined to pander to pharmaceutical-industry imperatives. As an added safeguard and as a condition of FDA certification, researchers and their institutions wouldn't be permitted to accept pharmaceutical company subsidies or sponsorships. And just as the volunteers or paid trial participants aren't told what specific drugs or treatments they are being given, the trial conductors wouldn't know which company is producing the drug being tested. Equally important, the results of the trials would belong to the US government and not Big Pharma. Physicians and researchers everywhere would be able to see and learn from the data.

By conducting its own clinical trials, the FDA would also have the freedom to design its own protocols. Approval would not be based only on whether taking the drug is better than taking a placebo, but whether the new drug is a significant improvement over previously approved drugs, time-tested treatments, and holistic therapies.

How do the risks and benefit of a new diabetes drug, for example, compare to a change in diet and moderate exercise? How does a new prescription pain reliever compare to taking an over-the-counter aspirin? Does a new cancer treatment extend a patient's life or simply mask the symptoms of the disease? How many years would it take a patient using a new osteoporosis drug to build enough bone density to warrant taking it?

You would logically think such basic questions are addressed in clinical trials, but they rarely are. One of the reasons is that the new "miracle" drugs don't measure up to industry claims, and the drug producer would rather the consumers and their physicians not know it. The drug companies also have no financial incentive to comparison test their products with traditional, centuries-old remedies or drugs that are no longer in patent, and hence cannot become the private property of the drug producer. For example, a change in diet for sufferers of psoriasis and other skin-related conditions may be a far more effective treatment than prescription topical ointments. Only you will not know this from drug-company-sponsored clinical trials.

Another advantage over the old system would be the huge cost savings and health benefits as a result of the decreasing number of "me too" drugs put on the market. The pharmaceutical companies would be less inclined to produce these copycat drugs because they would have to prove that their formulations are actually better than the ones they copied. The effort spent to produce such drugs could then be channeled into truly innovative research. Who knows? Maybe a renaissance in medical breakthroughs would result.

The pharmaceutical industry (as well as the politicians in its pocket) will naturally argue that the federal government ought to stay out of the business of conducting clinical research, that corporations can do the job more efficiently and less costly. Overwhelming evidence suggests otherwise. A recent survey has shown that university hospitals can perform drug trials that are more reliable and for an estimated one-tenth to one-twentieth of the cost of industry trials.[lxi] Beyond these advantages, there would be the added benefit of increased cash flow to academic institutions and medical professionals who presumably will be less engaged with reviewing suspect data than they will be producing their own reliable data.

How much would it cost the American taxpayer to empower the FDA to conduct clinical trials? One hospital researcher with extensive clinical trial experience has estimated that levying a 2 percent tax on prescription medication would quickly create a fund large enough to cover the entire process.[lxii] Several European governments accomplish the same thing by taxing the pharmaceutical industry itself.[lxiii] But whatever system is put into place to finance testing, the net results would cost considerably less than what consumers already pay in the form of inflated drug prices. This much we know for certain, thanks in no small part to price-fixing investigations. As we have seen, a pill costing the manufacturer a mere 11¢ to produce is routinely sold for $25. And the alleged $800 million or more that the industry routinely claims to put into research and development to develop a new drug is actually less than $100 million.[lxiv]

Clinical trials aside, there are plenty of other ways the system needs to be revamped. High on my list would be giving FDA regulators complete access to all corporate-sponsored drug tests and data associated with them. Further, FDA researchers should have access to pharmaceutical archives to mine the results of past trials. Such oversight of corporate records is routine for the

IRS. Why shouldn't other government regulators, such as the FDA, have access to Big Pharma's records? GlaxoSmithKline has promised this, and it may very well live up to its promise (though I am doubtful), but all the drug companies need to follow suit.

Transparency must be the rule, not the exception. Thankfully, the passage of the Sunshine Act, which is part of the Affordable Care Act and was put into effect in 2013, is a major step in the right direction. This act requires drug manufacturers and producers of medical devices and supplies to report payments, ownership, investment interests, and other transfers of value they make to physicians and teaching hospitals. You and I need only go to the CMS.gov website to see the potential conflicts of interest a physician might have. I would go the next logical step and mandate that drug companies also declare all payments, subsidies, and advertising that they give medical societies, groups, and associations, as occurred in Kentucky when NAMI was helping Eli Lilly keep Zyprexa on the preferred-drug list. If corporate sponsorship makes it possible for a society or association to host continuing education junkets at tropical resorts or expensive restaurants, such payments must be declared and the event ought to be called what it is: a sales conference.

Along these same lines, medical journals and other forms of medical knowledge dissemination must admit the disservice they are doing to the public by permitting obviously biased writers and accepting ghostwritten reviews and reports. As Dr. John Abramson from Harvard Medical School has pointed out, this shouldn't be a game of cat and mouse in which corporate sponsors do their best to hide the ways that their scientific results have been spun.[lxv] Medical journals in particular must adhere to far higher scientific standards because millions of lives hang in the balance. Doing otherwise will ultimately result in public disregard for physicians in general. Ethics promoter and former *New England Journal of Medicine* editor Dr. Jerome Kassirer stated this best: "At issue is whether the public can trust us not only to be at their side but on their side."[lxvi]

Another necessary reform would prohibit direct-to-consumer advertising of prescription drugs on television, radio, print media and on the Internet. Despite pronouncements to the contrary, it's simply delusional to believe that the purpose of these ads is to enliven discussion between a patient and his or her physician, as the ads purport to do. Their purpose is to sell drugs, which they do by lulling viewers into believing the medications they are being sold are safe and effective; otherwise, the companies wouldn't be advertising it. The bottom line is this: if the drugs were truly safe, they wouldn't require a prescription to sell them, and just because they have been approved by the FDA, it doesn't mean they're effective or safe. A consumer simply can't evaluate the efficacy of a particular drug in a thirty-second TV spot, which is why the practice is outlawed in all advanced countries except the United States and New Zealand. As the *New York Times* as has aptly put it, "Consumer advertising, delivered to the masses as a shotgun blast, rather than as specific information to concerned patients or caregivers, results in more prescriptions and less appropriate prescribing."[lxvii] That's why the drug companies do it and why it must be stopped.

New laws must also be in place to regulate the widespread practice of prescribing drugs off-label. If I had my way, the practice—with few exceptions—would be banned altogether. After all, if a drug hasn't been proven safe for a particular use, then it ought not be prescribed for that use. In certain life-or-death instances, however, or if a physician is convinced beyond any doubt that it is the right drug to prescribe to their patient at that time, then the physician ought to be permitted to prescribe it. However, he or she should rightfully first obtain a legal consent form signed by their patient as evidence that the patient is aware that they are being prescribed a drug that has not been approved by the FDA for that purpose and is also aware of the potential negative side effects (which could be listed on the consent form in easy-to-understand language). The emphasis here should be on physician responsibility and perhaps too, liability. Remember Gabriel Myers, who underwent examinations that lasted for two or three minutes before he was prescribed what turned out to be a deadly drug cocktail? If a physician believes he or she may have to explain to a jury why they made the decision, there would be fewer off-label prescriptions written.

Further, as we saw in the Austin Pledger story, had there been adequate labeling on drug packaging, there would likely not have been an off-label prescription written. Drug labels and packaging must clearly present all possible side effects—and I don't mean in print so small that a consumer must squint to read the individual words or written with such convoluted terminology and phrasing that even the doctors themselves are confused by what is being communicated. Manufacturers must be legally obligated to list all the potential side effects, which side effects are the most serious, and the percentages of individuals taking the drug who have suffered such side effects. Further, this information must be presented to both patient and physician—if not in a clearly and easily understood booklet accompanying each prescription, then in an electronic form available on the Internet.

Drug pricing is another long-overdue reform. Why is it that drugs are 50 percent less expensive in Europe? Why shouldn't Medicare and Medicaid comparison shop for the best drug prices? Why is a drug that once cost a consumer less than six dollars a day when it was under patent protection now cost consumers over one hundred dollars a day (when it is no longer under patent protection)? The answer to all of these questions is the same: drug companies selling their products in the United States can charge whatever price they want and know that our insurers and health care system will pay for it.

Thanks to drug industry-sponsored media hype, we are told that our health care providers must make all products available to everyone regardless of the price. Otherwise, we will have "death panels." Such a fallacy belies the overwhelming evidence from abroad. Health care systems in Europe and Canada (and Cuba too), which are more selective about the effectiveness of the drugs they permit to be marketed and invite competition into the equation, provide better health care and less-expensive drugs. The United States should do the same by demanding that the FDA raise its scientific standards, compel financial regulators to put a stop to price-fixing, and motivate legislators to level the playing field by putting a stop to the many special interest rules and regulations that are voted into law every year.

Next on my overhaul agenda would be holding drug companies and their executives accountable for breaking the rules. I do not mean just leveling a fine, for clearly a financial penalty is not enough. The chief executives of these companies will continue to commit illegal or unethical acts and encourage their subordinates to do the same as the "cost of doing business" until they themselves are held criminally accountable.

A surefire way to move this reform forward is to remove immunity from prosecution as a bargaining chip in cases involving criminal activities such as medical fraud, lying to federal officials, bribery, and failure to disclose life-threatening adverse effects. Those engaged in wrongdoing need to be held personally liable and face federal prison for their crimes. Because of the decisions these executives make—oftentimes driven by the tens of millions of dollars in bonus compensation they receive—people die. That's manslaughter. Don't issue these criminals a "get out of jail free" card because they can afford to buy one.

I would go even further in this regard: if a company and its executives are serial offenders, not only should the chief officers go to jail but the company should also forfeit future profits or patent rights to some or all of the drugs it is producing. In particularly egregious instances, I would go to the extreme of issuing a corporate death penalty. By this, I mean the charters giving corporations license to operate should be revoked. This is not only legally feasible, but it's morally justified when many hundreds and potentially millions of people are harmed because scientific data has been manipulated or marketers are knowingly bringing an inferior and dangerous product to market. Although I will be the first to admit that charter revocation hasn't yet been applied to multinational corporate lawbreakers the way it has commonly been used to hold small companies liable for injurious behavior, I don't see any reason not to try. Loyola Law School professor Robert Benson attempted to do this to Union Oil of California (Unocal) in the aftermath of a massive oil spill and numerous wanton acts of pollution in the 1960s. If Unocal's charter had been revoked, perhaps BP would have taken greater precautions and there wouldn't have been the 2010 Deepwater Horizon oil spill in the Gulf of Mexico.

"People mistakenly assume that we have to try to control these giant corporate repeat offenders...[only with fines] but the law has always allowed the attorney general to go to court to simply dissolve a corporation for wrongdoing and sell its assets to others who will operate in the public interest," Professor Benson wrote. "Baseball players and convicted individuals in California get only three strikes. Why should big corporations get endless strikes?"[lxviii]

Pharmaceutical chieftains will claim that their companies are too large and too important to be dissolved. The health of the nation depends on them. But consider, if you will, how twisted this logic actually is. It's similar to saying we must tolerate criminal behavior as the price for our own (ill) health. The truth of the matter is that we don't have to tolerate injustice. Nor do we need worry that our continued health depends upon these corporations. Any lifesaving or life-enhancing medications these companies produce can, by court order, be turned over to others for generic drug production.

The greater challenge is mustering the political will necessary to bring about such changes. Simply accomplishing a single one of them, such as making all drug studies and the data associated with them available to the FDA or putting criminal offenders behind bars, would be enough to bring significant improvements. But the problem here is the close relationship between the drug manufacturers and government legislators.

Data compiled by the Center for Responsive Politics and commissioned by the Union of Concerned Scientists show that between 1998 and 2013, pharmaceutical and health-product manufacturers spent nearly $3 billion on lobbying our lawmakers, making them the single largest contributor to legislative efforts than any other industry.[lxix] Of the more than one thousand registered pharmaceutical lobbyists last year, over twenty are former members of Congress, and one former key player in the health care debate was paid over $11 million in salary by the pharmaceutical industry.[lxx] And while we're talking big numbers, between 2009 and 2011, prescription drug, biotechnology, and medical device companies spent more than $700 million specifically lobbying Congress and the White House.[lxxi] That's the equivalent of spending over $1 million dollars for each congressman and senator on Capitol Hill!

Such huge sums cause one to ask, what are the pharmaceutical chieftains getting in return for their investments? Among the most obvious benefits are predatory pricing practices, which include bans on the importation of certified generic pharmaceuticals (at a fraction of American prices) and a provision that prevents Medicare and Medicaid to find the best prices for the billions they have to spend on drugs. Then, of course, there are the Big Pharma alumni appointments to government regulatory advisory boards. I've previously mentioned the former executives at both Lilly and J&J on such boards, but the sad truth is that there are so many others that, as one insider remarked, it would be difficult to find anyone with authority who wasn't connected in some way to the corporations they seek to regulate.

Equally alarming are the industry-friendly legislative proposals that routinely go before the House and Senate. In the past year alone, I have seen initiatives that would erode the FDA's standard of substantial evidence when reviewing drugs and medical devices, legislation that would relax conflict-of-interest standards for federal advisory members at the FDA, and the restricting of whistleblower statutes. Then, there is legislation under consideration that could reasonably be called the "Stop Stephen A. Sheller Bill." This would restrict the ability of state attorney generals to partner with plaintiff attorneys. Imagine the consequences if such legislation is passed. It was precisely because of the partnerships I made with state attorneys that we successfully took on Big Tobacco and the pharmaceutical giants.

Make no mistake: the business of health care is big business, not health care. This is why pharmaceutical companies are not only funding the political campaigns of our senators and congressmen, but they're also working on state and local levels to fund the campaigns of judges who will likely be more receptive to their company's interests. Spearheading the so-called judicial "reform" movement is the secretive Civil Justice Reform Group (CJRG), which is comprised of the general counsels of some of the largest and most profitable corporations in the world. Among the group representatives are Aetna, AT&T, BP, Bristol-Myers Squibb, Chevron, Chrysler, Citibank, DuPont, Exxon, Ford, General Electric, General Motors, GlaxoSmithKline, Koch Cos., Merck & Co., Pfizer, Procter & Gamble, State Farm, Texaco, W. R. Grace, and, you guessed it, J&J. As one reporter has aptly pointed out, these companies are responsible for at least one or more products or services that have recently harmed or killed Americans, and not a single chief executive was seriously investigated or went to jail. Remember Merck's Vioxx, W. R. Grace's asbestos products, Ford's exploding Pinto, and BP's oil spill in the Gulf of Mexico? Corporate executives knew of the dangers yet continued to sell the products or services to unsuspecting consumers.[lxxii] Now we can add Janssen's Risperdal to the list.

Sadly, conditions may have to get considerably worse before they can get better. This appears to be the case in my own hometown of Philadelphia, where thanks to lobbying efforts, corporate profits are taking precedence over the sick and needy. For nearly as long as I can remember, competent Philadelphia judges kept both the courthouse doors open to injured individuals and cases moving forward in a timely way. Now, it appears, judges are under tacit orders to make it more difficult for plaintiffs to bring cases, to receive fair compensation for injuries, or to punish wrongdoing corporations by assessing punitive damages. Their ultimate objective is that corporations should be let off the hook when their products harm or kill their customers. As a commenter for the Pennsylvania Association for Justice has said, "If changes to the courts are good news to a group funded by Big Tobacco, insurance companies, and pharmaceutical firms... is that good news for anyone else?"[lxxiii]

This brings me back to where I started: the disputed Bush versus Gore election and what more I could and should have done to demand that justice was served. Democracy is not a spectator sport. Not until we exercise our rights and move others to awareness and to action can we protect the Gabriel Meyerses of the world. He and countless others injured by the pharmaceutical industry aren't the only victims of the fraud. All of us are. Do not become one of the many who will look back on what has happened and ask, "What were we thinking? How could this possibly have all come about?" Rather, look back and be proud of what you did to be a voice of conscience and justice in a time when we need conscience and justice more desperately than we need the next "miracle" drug.

Acknowledgments

Clarence Darrow once said, "As long as the world shall last, there will be wrongs, and if no man rebelled, those wrongs would last forever."

I thank the many men and women who inherently follow this principle and have set higher standards for seeking justice with integrity. Early on in my life, Dr. Thomas G. Lawrence, my science teacher from Erasmus Hall High School in Brooklyn, and Drs. Marvin Wolfgang and John Honnold, professors at the University of Pennsylvania, taught me the value of seeking truth with integrity through science and law.

As a young lawyer, Reverend Paul Washington's tenacity to protect all people and do what is right with integrity despite being challenged greatly encouraged me. Judges Edmund Spaeth, Raymond Pace Alexander, and Alexander Barbieri set the standard that enabled me to understand how the judiciary and legal system can protect our citizens with justice in the most difficult situations.

I owe gratitude to Judges Sandra Mazur Moss and William Manfredi for being loyal and consistent friends and sounding boards over many years of my legal practice, keeping me on the straight and narrow. I thank former Governor Edward Rendell for demonstrating how good political leadership can result in justice, and for advancing hope and benefit for the majority of citizens.

Fellow attorneys who worked with me on these various cases, Mike Mustokoff, Mark Lipowicz, Mark Aronchick, Teresa Cavenagh, Michael Freedland, and Gary Farmer, added so much to my analysis of what could be done and the success of what we accomplished. Our Risperdal litigation partner Tom Kline continues to seek justice for our individual Risperdal gynecomastia clients.

Steven Brill's 15-part "docu-serial" 'America's Most Admired Lawbreaker' published by the Huffington Post's Highline division delves deeply into the history of Johnson and Johnson's marketing of Risperdal. I thank him for his dedication to providing the journalistic expose and appreciate his including me in the narrative

A special note of thanks to Valerie Jones for her integral role in shaping this manuscript including delving into, researching and finding documents and materials that would elude most investigative reporters. Her wise counsel and invaluable input are on every page. Also a shout out to Christopher Naughton, former prosecutor, trial attorney and host of the Emmy award-winning television program *The American Law Journal,* for providing a forum in which consumer protection, constitutional rights and so many of the issues dear to my heart can be openly discussed and debated.

Dr. David Kessler, past commissioner of the FDA, joined me early on in my career in the tobacco fight and has been forthright in standing up to justice in the pharmaceutical litigation.

Bobbie Mitnik, my wife's mother, was also a tenacious champion of doing what's right. Her unwillingness to accept injustice on any level was what led me to call the state of Florida to task over the troubled butterfly ballot.

Equally courageous have been my many clients—to name a few who inspire me even today, I thank Benita Pledger, Victoria Starr, and James Wetta for their unwavering commitment to justice and integrity for themselves, their families, and all families, despite the hardships they met with in the process.

Finally, I thank the unwavering support and love of my family, who understands my passion for justice and carries the torch with me: my wife, Sandy and my daughters, Jamie, Mimi, Danielle, and Lauren. My hope is that their children, my grandchildren—Dane, Beau, Ally, Eve, and Hudson—will continue the quest.

About Sidney D. Kirkpatrick

SIDNEY D. KIRKPATRICK IS THE *New York Times* best-selling author of six critically acclaimed nonfiction books:

A CAST OF KILLERS
TURNING THE TIDE
LORDS OF SIPAN
EDGAR CAYCE: AN AMERICAN PROPHET
THE REVENGE OF THOMAS EAKINS
HITLER'S HOLY RELICS
TRUE TALES FROM THE EDGAR CAYCE ARCHIVES

Notes

i   "Gabriel Myers DCF Report," 2009, http://www.dcf.state. fl.us/initiatives/GMWorkgroup/docs/GMPresentation. pdf.

ii   Ibid.

iii   Ibid.

iv   "The Real Lesson of Columbine: Psychiatric Drugs Induce Violence," Citizens Commission on Human Rights of Colorado, April 20, 2011, http://psychiatricfraud. org/2011/04/the-real-lesson-of-columbine-psychiatric-drugs-induce-violence/.

v   Evelyn Pringle, "FDA Throws Lifeline to Antipsychotic Pushers," *Counterpunch*, June 12, 2009.

vi   Alice Mundy, *Dispensing with the Truth* (New York: St. Martin's Press, 2001), 52.

vii   2006–2013, Vitals.com & MDX Medical, Doctor Reviews, http://www.vitals.com/doctors/Dr_Sohail_Punjwani/profile.

viii   Martin Merzer, *The Miami Herald Report: Democracy Held Hostage* (New York: St. Martin's Press, 2001), 7.

ix   George Bennett and Marc Caputo, "Voting-Machine Errors Discovered Four Years Ago," *Palm Beach Post*, December 8, 2000, https://www.mail-archive.com/ctrl@listserv.aol.com/msg56438.html.

x   Martin Merzer, *The Miami Herald Report: Democracy Held Hostage*, (New York: St. Martin's Press, (May 2001), 78.

xi   Steven Foster, *The Judiciary, Civil Liberties and Human Rights* (Edinburgh, Scotland: Edinburgh University Press, 2006), 80.

xii   Richard Neumann, "Conflicts of Interest in *Bush v. Gore*: Did Some Justices Vote Illegally?" *Georgetown Journal of Legal Ethics* (16 Geo. J. Legal Ethics 375, 2003), http://scholarlycommons.law.hofstra.edu/cgi/viewcontent.cgi?article=1117&context=faculty_scholarship, 375.

xiii   David DeGraw, "The Richest 1% Have Captured America's Wealth—What's It Going to Take to Get It Back?:" Part II of "The Economic Elite vs. People of the USA,'" *Alternet*, February 16, 2010, http://www.alternet.org/story/145705/the_richest_1_have_captured_america's_wealth_--_what's_it_going_to_take_to_get_it_back.

xiv   "Growing Apart," *The Economist*, September 21, 2013, http://www.economist.com/news/leaders/21586578-americas-income-inequality-growing-again-time-cut-subsidies-rich-and-invest.

xv   Jeff Gerth, "Bush Tried to Sway a Tax Rule Change But Then Withdrew," *New York Times*, May 19, 1982. http://www.nytimes.com/1982/05/19/business/bush-tried-to-sway-a-tax-rule-change-but-then-withdrew.html?pagewanted=all

xvi   Union of Concerned Scientists: FDA Scientists Survey (2006), http://www.ucsusa.org/our-work/center-science-and-democracy/promoting-scientific-integrity/summary-of-the-fda-scientist.html#.ViKuuRCrRYd.

xvii   Tom Watkins, "Papers Indicate Firm Knew Possible Prozac Suicide Risk," *CNN*, January 3, 2005, http://www.cnn.com/2005/HEALTH/01/03/prozac.documents/index.html\.

xviii Richard Zitrin and Carol M. Langford, *The Moral Compass of the American Lawyer: Truth, Justice, Power and Greed* (New York: Ballantine Books, 1999), 193-203. https://docs.google.com/document/d/1NV3oZYf85funkFTy7wy15T1-U9n3bzkBMZ7ltZrQCYw/edit).

xix Adam Liptak, "Free Prozac in the Junk Mail Draws a Lawsuit, *New York Times*, July 6, 2002, http://www.nytimes.com/2002/07/06/us/free-prozac-in-the-junk-mail-draws-a-lawsuit.html.

xx Office of the White House Press Secretary, November 25, 2002, http://georgewbush-whitehouse.archives.gov/news/releases/2002/11/20021125-6.html.

xxi Katie Thomas, "A Data Trove Now Guides Drug Pitches," *New York Times*, May 17, 2013, http://www.nytimes.com/2013/05/17/business/a-data-trove-now-guides-drug-company-pitches.html?_r=0.

xxii Molly Merrill, "Hospitals 'Struggling' to Protect Patient Data," *Health Care IT News*, November 8, 2010, http://www.healthcareitnews.com/news/hospitals-struggling-protect-patient-data?page=1.

xxiii Marcia Angell, *The Truth about the Drug Companies: How They Deceive Us and What To Do about It* (New York: Random House, 2004), p. 305.

xxiv Kevin O'Reilly, "Quantifying Adverse Drug Events: Med Mishaps Send Millions Back for Care," *American Medical News*, June 13, 2011, http://www.amednews.com/article/20110613/profession/306139944/2/.

xxv   J. Lazaro et al. and F.H. Gurwitz et al., "Why Learn about Adverse Drug Reactions (ADR)?" Institute of Medicine, National Academy Press, 2000, http://www.fda.gov/Drugs/DevelopmentApprovalProcess/DevelopmentResources/DrugInteractionsLabeling/ucm114848.html.

xxvi The study was published in Archives of Internal Medicine. It was funded by the National Library of Medicine and the Regenstrief Institute, a nonprofit health care research organization affiliated with the Indiana University School of Medicine.

xxvii Sovereign Health Sponsored *Psychguides.com*, http://www.psychguides.com/guides/shopping-addiction-treatment-program-options/.

xxviii Robert Whitaker, *Anatomy of An Epidemic* (New York: Broadway Books, 2010), 113.

xxix Joseph Glenmullen, MD, *The Antidepressant Solution* (New York: Free Press, 2006), electronic edition, Chapter 1, Antidepressant Withdrawal and Dependence.

xxx   "2012 National Business Ethics Survey," *Ethics Resource Center*, http://www.ethics.org/nbes/.
See also: Erika Kelton, "The Case Against GE, New Report Shows Real Motive for Attacks on SEC Program," http://www.forbes.com/sites/erikakelton/2012/06/06/whistleblower-case-against-ge-new-report-show-real-motives-for-attacks-on-sec-program/.
A fine introduction to this subject can be found in "The Complete Guide to Snitching," Christopher Matthews, *Wall Street Journal*, December 15, 2011, http://blogs.wsj.com/corruption-currents/2011/12/15/the-complete-guide-to-snitching/.

xxxi   Miriam Hill, "Whistle-blower's perspective on Lilly case," *Philadelphia Inquirer*, January 19, 2009, http://www.psychologydebunked.com/email0902_Lillywhistleblower.htm.

xxxii   Gardiner Harris, "States Try to Limit Drugs in Medicaid, But Makers Resist," *New York Times*, December 18, 2003, http://www.nytimes.com/2003/12/18/business/states-try-to-limit-drugs-in-medicaid-but-makers-resist.html.

xxxiii   Ken Silverstein, "Prozac.org," *Mother Jones*, November/December 1999, http://www.motherjones.com/politics/1999/11/prozacorg.

xxxiv Martha Rosenberg, "Should Your Child Be on Drugs? Yes Says Big Pharma," *Intrepid Report*, October 1, 2012, http://www.intrepidreport.com/archives/7512.

xxxv Jim Edwards, "Pfizer Paid for Doc's Helicopter in Off-Label Geodon Push, Suit Claims," *CBS Money Watch*, September 17, 2009, http://www.cbsnews.com/news/pfizer-paid-for-docs-helicopter-in-off-label-geodon-push-suit-claims/.

xxxvi New Freedom Commission Report, http://www2.nami.org/Content/NavigationMenu/Inform_Yourself/About_Public_Policy/New_Freedom_Commission/Goal_4_Early_Mental_Health_Screening.htm.

xxxvii State of Texas ex rel. Jones v. Janssen LP, D- 1GV-04-001288, District Court, Travis County, Texas.

xxxviii CBS Moneywatch, "WebMD's Depression Test Has Only One (Sponsored) Answer: You're "At Risk.", February 22, 2010, http://www.cbsnews.com/news/webmds-depression-test-has-only-one-sponsored-answer-youre-at-risk/

xxxix Martha Rosenberg, OpEdNews.com, "Grassley Investigates Lilly/WebMD link Reported by Washington Post," February 24, 2010, http://www.opednews.com/articles/Grassley-Investigates-Lill-by-Martha-Rosenberg-100224-629.html.

xl   Dr. Joseph Mercola, "WeMD, the Latest Shill for Monsanto," Online newsletter, January 16, 2016, http://articles.mercola.com/sites/articles/archive/2016/01/19/webmd-monsanto-gmo.aspx.

xli   From WebMD's own announcement: Daniel DeNoon, "FDA, WebMD Announce Partnership," December 3, 2008, http://www.webmd.com/news/20081203/fda-webmd-announce-partnership.

xlii   Milt Freudenheim, Business Technology; Seeking Safer Treatments for Schizophrenia, *New York Times*, January 1, 21015, http://www.nytimes.com/1992/01/15/business/business-technology-seeking-safer-treatments-for-schizophrenia.html.

xliii   Risperdal advertisement by Janssen in the *American Journal of Psychiatry*, volume 151 (1994): A111.

xliv   FDA warning letters: http://www.fda.gov/downloads/Drugs/GuidanceComplianceRegulatoryInformation/EnforcementActivitiesbyFDA/WarningLettersand-NoticeofViolationLetterstoPharmaceutical-Companies/ucm055315.pdf.

xlv   Joseph Biederman biography *Source Watch*, http://www.sourcewatch.org/index.php/Joseph_Biederman.

xlvi Dr. Joseph Mercola, "How Can a 4000% Increase in Bipolar Disorder Be Possible?" Online newsletter, July 30, 2011, http://articles.mercola.com/sites/articles/archive/2011/07/30/why-did-bipolar-disorder-increase-40x-over-last-ten-years.aspx.

xlvii Biederman deposition: http://highline.huffingtonpost.com/miracleindustry/americas-most-admired-lawbreaker/assets/documents/8/biederman-depo.pdf.

xlviii Rachel Ewing, "In Utero Exposure to Antidepressants May Influence Autism Risk," Drexel NOW News Release, http://drexel.edu/now/archive/2014/June/Antidepressants-Autism-Risk/.

xlix Kelly Patricia O'Meara, "Honey, They Shrunk My Brain-Study Confirms Antipsychotics Decrease Brain Tissue," CCHR International, The Mental Health Watchdog, http://www.cchrint.org/2013/09/12/honey-they-shrunk-my-brain-study-confirms-antipsychotics-decrease-brain-tissue/.

l Research report: "Top FDA Officials Compromised by Conflicts of Interest," Alliance For Human Research Protection, November 9, 2009, http://ahrp.org/top-fda-officials-compromised-by-conflicts-of-interest/.

li Ibid.

lii   Michael Bobelian, "J&J's $2.2 Billion Settlement Won't Stop Big Pharma's Addiction To Off-Label Sales," *Forbes*, November 12, 1913, http://www.forbes.com/sites/michaelbobelian/2013/11/12/jjs-2-2-billion-settlement-wont-stop-big-pharmas-addiction-to-off-label-sales/.

liii   Boycott.com Campaign: http://buycott.com/campaign/707/boycott-the-band-aid-america-s-1-bandage-brand.

liv   David Voreacos and Alex Nussbaum, "J&J Directors Ignored 'Red Flags' on recalls, Probes, Suit Says," *Bloomberg*, December 22, 2010, http://www.bloomberg.com/news/articles/2010-12-21/j-j-directors-accused-by-shareholders-of-ignoring-warnings-before-recalls.

lv   Lorraine Bailey, "Johnson & Johnson CEO 'Grossly' Overpaid As Firm's Reputation Took a Beating, Suit Says," July 19, 2012, *Courthouse News*, http://www.cnssecurities-law.com/2012/07/19/458.htm.

lvi   R. L. Findling, et al., "Prolactin Levels During Long-Term Risperidone Treatment in Children and Adolescents," *Journal of Clinical Psychiatry*, v. 64(11) November, 2003, pp.1362-9, http://www.ncbi.nlm.nih.gov/pubmed/14658952.

lvii   Paul Basken, "Major Fraud Plea Has University Scientists Regretting Journal Article, Chronicle of Higher Education, November 20, 2013,

http://chronicle.com/blogs/percolator/major-fraud-plea-has-university-scientists-regretting-journal-article/33713.

lviii Paul Basken, "Major Fraud Plea Has University Scientists Regretting Journal Article, Chronicle of Higher Education, November 20, 2013, http://chronicle.com/blogs/percolator/major-fraud-plea-has-university-scientists-regretting-journal-article/33713.

lix Alicia Mundy and Jared A. Favole, "FDA Scientists Ask Obama To Restructure Drug Agency," *Wall Street Journal*, January 8, 2009, http://www.wsj.com/articles/SB123142562104564381.

lx Eric Lichtblau and Scott Shane, "Vast FDA Effort Tracked E-Mails of Its Scientists," *New York Times*, July 14, 2012, http://www.nytimes.com/2012/07/15/us/fda-surveillance-of-scientists-spread-to-outside-critics.html?_r=0.

lxi Bassand J-P, Martyin, Ryden L., et al., "The Need for Resources for Clinical Research," *Lancet* 360 (2002): 1866–9.

lxii Peter Gotzche, *Deadly Medicines and Organized Crime* (Oxford: Radcliffe Medical Press, 2013), electronic edition.

lxiii Ibid.

lxiv Merrill Goozner, *The 800 Million Pill* (Oakland: University of California Press, 2005) 237, 239.

lxv   John Abramson, *Overdosed America: The Broken Promise of American Medicine* (New York: Harper Collins, 2008) 242.

lxvi   Dr. Jerome Kassirer, *On The Take: How Medicine's Complicity With big Business Can endanger Your Health* (Oxford University Press, 2005) 213.

lxvii Kurt Strange, "Consumer Drug Advertising Should Be Banned," *New York Times*, December 16, 2013, **http://www. nytimes.com/roomfordebate/2013/12/15/is-the-drug-industry-developing-cures-or-hyping-up-demand/ consumer-drug-advertising-should-be-banned**.

lxviii Russell Mokhiber, "The Death Penalty for Corporations Comes of Age," *Business Ethics*, November 1, 1998, http:// www.corpwatch.org/article.php?id=1810.

lxix   Top Spenders List "Open Secrets," Center for Responsive Politics, 1998-2015, http://www.opensecrets.org/lobby/top. php?showYear=2013&indexType=i.

lxx   Alex Wayne and Drew Armstrong, "Tauzin's $11.6 Million Made Him Highest-Paid Health-Law Lobbyist," *Bloomberg Business*, November 29, 2011, http://www.bloomberg.com/ news/articles/2011-11-29/tauzin-s-11-6-million-made-him-highest-paid-health-law-lobbyist.

lxxi   Research report "Drug and Medical Device Companies Have Outsized Influence on FDA," Center for Science and

Democracy, Union of Concerned Scientists, March 28, 2012, http://www.ucsusa.org/scientific_integrity/solutions/ agency-specific_solutions/drug-companies-influence-FDA.html.

lxxii   Wayne Parsons, "Reclaiming Justice: Battling Tort 'Reform," *Trial Magazine*, The American Association for Justice, December 2012, http://www.takejusticeback.com/sites/default/ files/AAJ%20Trial%20The%20web%20of%20 tort%20%E2%80%98reform%E2%80%99.pdf.

lxxiii   News Release "Philadelphia's Removal from 'Judicial Hellhole' List: Who Cares...," Pennsylvania Association for Justice, December 12, 2012, http://communityvoices. post-gazette.com/all-categories/item/35225-philadelphia-s-removal-from-judicial-hellhole-list-who-cares-what-front.

CPSIA information can be obtained
at www.ICGtesting.com
Printed in the USA
LVOW10s0118281216

518910LV00007B/195/P

9 780615 893167